Community Care and the Voluntary Sector

The Role of Voluntary Organisations in a Changing World

Paul Reading

Published by
VENTURE PRESS
16 Kent Street
Birmingham
B5 6RD
Tel. 021 622 3911

First Published 1994

Community Care and the Voluntary Sector

Paul Reading

British Library Cataloguing-in-Publication Data.
A catalogue record for this book is available from the British Library.

ISBN 1 873878 15X (paperback)

Printed and bound in Great Britain by
Biddles Ltd, Guildford and King's Lynn

Contents

To Marilyn

Acknowledgements

A wide range of people have helped to bring this book to fruition, notably the executive committee, staff and day centre members associated with Oxford MIND, a very special voluntary organisation. Of all these individuals the key person has been Jane Hope, consistent, creative and positive in all that she does.

In the early stages of the project I had particularly useful conversations and communications with Simon Hebditch at NCVO, Gordon Lishman of Age Concern, Keith Hawley, then working for Oxfordshire Social Services Department, and Marilyn Taylor from SAUS at Bristol University.

At Oxford Brookes University my colleagues Clare Gillies and Peter Bradley have provided unfailing friendship and support. Tracey Molloy has been efficient and quick in typing the manuscript. Jo Campling has quietly encouraged my efforts with patience and understanding.

The most significant help has come from Marilyn Taylor, Team Leader in a hard working voluntary organisation in Winchester. Her support, persistence and humour have encouraged me to believe that the book was worth writing.

1
Community care and the voluntary sector – setting the scene

A number of words and associations come to mind in trying to describe the purpose of this chapter, none of which is sufficient in their own right. It is both an introduction and an overview and it is a sketch-map of two overlapping landscapes which are both separate yet mutually dependent. Voluntary organisations are part of community care but are involved in a lot more besides social welfare. Community care needs voluntary sector involvement but has a vast range of informal, statutory and commercial activity which does not involve voluntary organisations.

A starting-point is to describe and define the terms voluntary organisation and community care. This is followed by an examination of the variety of voluntary organisations: their size, scope, history and role in society. The strengths and weaknesses of the voluntary sector are discussed with an emphasis on the challenges such strengths and weaknesses produce. It is important to put the picture that emerges into both a political and social policy context in order to be realistic about what can be achieved in this field. The book is based on some underlying principles as well as the author's personal and political values and these are made explicit as a prelude to an outline of the book as a whole.

DEFINITIONS

Defining the terms voluntary organisation and community care is fraught with difficulty. This is because the terms themselves are vague, and because understanding them depends upon your particular perspective. As a middle-aged, white, male lecturer in social work I will probably see them differently from a young, black, female member of a self-help group.

Voluntary organisations

In defining the term voluntary organisations three categories are used: what they are, what they are not, and what they may be.

Voluntary organisations – What they are:

- Self-governing associations of people who have joined together to take action for communal benefit.
- Organisations founded on voluntary effort.
- A force in society that provides social integration, cohesion and sense of identity.
- A critical voice able to develop a creative tension between community need, social policies, and service provision.
- Interactive bodies of people who expect to receive some benefit from their participation in the organisation.

Voluntary organisations – What they are not:

- Bodies established by statute, or part of local or central government.
- Agencies set up for financial gain.
- Altruistic organisations that expect no benefit for themselves.

Voluntary organisations – What they may be:

- Organisations which may employ staff.
- Bodies which may obtain income from statutory sources.
- Associations which may be registered as a charity.

Of 350,000 voluntary organisations in the UK, over 160,000 are registered as charities. Others are small unregistered groups, or they may be Friendly Societies or registered companies which have chosen not to seek charitable status.

In pulling apart the definition of voluntary organisations in this way it is recognised that no such organisation is perfect, nor is it easy to describe, understand and come to a common agreement about all the features mentioned. The voluntary sector is not static but is changing and developing all the time.

Community care

Defining community care seems even more difficult than defining voluntary organisations. There are many definitions from a variety of perspectives, and a crucial distinction is whether the perspective is optimistic or pessimistic. One classical definition has to be included because it sums up the dilemma so well:

> To the politician community care is a useful piece of rhetoric; to the sociologist it is a stick to beat institutional care with; to the civil servant it is a cheap alternative to institutional care which can be passed to local authorities for action – or inaction; to the visionary it is a dream of the new society in which people really do care; to social services departments it is a nightmare of heightened public expectations and inadequate resources to meet them. We are only just beginning to find out what it means to the old, the chronic sick and the handicapped.

> (Jones *et al*, 1978).

Such a definition wears surprisingly well considering that it was written a decade before the *Griffiths Report* (1988) and the National Health Service and Community Care Act (1990).

A general aim seems to be to maintain an individual's link with family, friends, and their own community through the provision of both informal care and formal services

In order to achieve this a number of principles of community care can be identified:

- Services should be planned and tailored to meet individual need.

- Consumers of services should be actively involved in such planning.

- Carers should be supported in their role and involved in any decision-making.

- Services should be as locally based as possible.

- Services should be as ordinary and as informally arranged as possible.

3

- Formal agencies should co-operate and work in partnership with each other.

There is an underlying assumption in these principles that sufficient resources of money, staff and buildings will be available. Statutory bodies are expected to act as enablers and purchasers of services as well as being direct providers. Voluntary organisations are expected to be providers of services as well as critics, campaigners and watchdogs.

Community care and the Black community

Finally under the heading of definitions it is important to stress the perception of community care by black communities. The need to identify with people from the same culture, the fear of racism and the history of services being geared to the white population mean that community care has a different meaning.

> The concept of community care is not a new one in the black communities. Historically, services for black communities have been unavailable, unacceptable, inadequate and inappropriate, forcing black families and community organisations to take on the task of meeting care needs.

(LGIU, 1991)

Identifying with and being supported by people from the same race and culture may be more clearly seen as community care than services defined as health care, social services, income support, or housing.

> Most black organisations deal with all aspects of community needs rather than dealing only with a specific need. Even those black organisations dealing only with a specific need such as mental health or disability operate within the framework of a comprehensive approach (responding to other needs such as housing, employment, education and so on) instead of compartmentalising and categorising 'special' needs.

(Ahmad, 1990)

DIVERSITY

The voluntary sector is nothing if not diverse. From large national charities with incomes of over £2 million per year to small self-help groups with no income at all. In describing this diversity it is important to make a distinction between the voluntary sector as a whole and voluntary organisations in particular. Many individuals take part in voluntary activity in the community care field but are not involved with any organisation. Such people may do so because they choose to (what Heginbotham refers to as 'pure' voluntary activity), and some because they feel obliged to (voluntary activity as a 'duty') (Heginbotham, 1990).

The number of people who take part in such individual activities is surprising given the overall media portrayal of our society. From TV adverts we look like a nation of healthy, lively, independent people whose only phobia is getting the stains and odours out of our clothes. In fact one adult in eight (approximately 3.5 million people), cares for a severely disabled relative at home (Central Statistical Office, 1989). While acknowledging the significance of this huge number of individuals, this book is not about them. It is about the people who are involved with the voluntary sector in a more organised way.

The National Council for Voluntary Organisations found it helpful to distinguish four broad areas of activity undertaken by voluntary organisations. These are: service provision, self-help or mutual aid, advocacy and campaigning, intermediary bodies. Some organisations concentrate on just one of these activities, others may be involved with several.

Service provision

At a local level voluntary organisations frequently put the bulk of their time, energy and money into providing a specific service. This may be a day centre run by a nationally known agency such as Age Concern, or a club for lonely people set up by an individual who has highlighted a local need. Such services include housing and sheltered accommodation, day care, advice and information, support for relatives, transport and counselling.

Self-help or mutual aid

The range of self-help and mutual support groups is enormous. Some, such as the Sickle Cell Disease Self-Help Group, are very small and only found in particular communities, whilst others, such as Gingerbread, have grown to be national bodies with groups all over the country. Such groups frequently start because there is little sympathy in society at large for the particular problem experienced, and they create an opportunity for consumers to be directly involved in both providing and receiving a service.

Advocacy and campaigning

This is the cutting-edge of the voluntary sector both in providing a voice for individuals and in presenting social issues to a local or national audience. MIND is a good example of an organisation that undertakes both these tasks, offering support to individuals and relatives at tribunals and inquests, as well as running campaigns on mental health issues.

Intermediary bodies

These organisations provide co-ordination, information and support to groups and agencies undertaking the three functions described above. Locally they are usually referred to as Councils for Voluntary Service or Voluntary Action. Nationally there is the National Council for Voluntary Organisations (NCVO) which takes the lead in debating social policy issues, assists other organisations in improving their effectiveness, and identifies the need for new voluntary action. Other umbrella bodies can be found in more specific fields such as the Standing Conference of Ethnic Minority Senior Citizens or the National Council of Voluntary Child Care Organisations.

Diversity may be an attractive quality in one respect, but it does not guarantee universal coverage of a particular social problem nor the quality or scale of the service provided. In 1990 NCVO had 575 national members, approximately half of which could be said to be involved with community care (NCVO, *Annual Review 1989/90*). Locally, even small Councils for Voluntary Action can boast membership of 150-plus (Oxfordshire CVA, *Annual Report 1990*). Within those impressive figures the scale and scope of the different organisations varies greatly. One study of self-help groups in Liverpool found that membership of such groups varied from 12 for a

Congenital Dislocation of the Hip Support Group to 2000 for a Colostomy Welfare Group (Campion *et al*, 1988).

DISTINCTIVENESS

As with the notion of diversity the concept of distinctiveness covers a multitude of sins. In using it to describe voluntary organisations three features are explored: strengths, weaknesses and challenges.

Strengths of voluntary organisations

Historically the Labour Party has been ambivalent about voluntary organisations, so it is surprising to find Labour Party documents outlining their strengths so clearly. A consultation document identifies nine 'specific advantages' which are:

1 a capacity to innovate, experiment and test new ideas;

2 flexibility, and the ability to respond quickly to changing needs;

3 good community links;

4 the ability to take risk;

5 cost-effectiveness, arising from their ability to target on very specific groups, localities or issues;

6 the capacity to promote change, challenge vested interests and campaign for improved services;

7 the opportunity to involve members of the community in planning and monitoring services;

8 the status to act as advocates for particular groups;

9 the potential to give people a sense of power and influence over the decisions which affect their lives.

(Labour Party Consultation Document, 1990)

Although this list is comprehensive it is important to add that independence from statutory requirements is an additional strength. From a commercial point of view another positive feature is that voluntary organisations are not required to make a profit.

Weaknesses of voluntary organisations

Most reports, discussion documents and policy initiatives concentrate on the positives, but it is also important to be realistic and note the limitations of voluntary organisations. Some of these are the opposite position from the strengths highlighted above. The following six points are worth noting:

1 the lack of statutory power or authority;

2 dependence on the goodwill of statutory agencies both local and national;

3 the prevalence of insecure funding;

4 small organisations may lack an organisational and management base;

5 the possibility of narrow thinking and inter-agency rivalry;

6 limited opportunities for training.

In addition it is clear that some voluntary organisations are more popular than others, both with regards to charitable giving and in the political and public support they experience. This is neatly highlighted by the director of the Mental Health Foundation who is quoted as saying 'Every year I try to push up the charity league table, and every year the donkey sanctuary is at least 10 places ahead of us' (quoted in Taylor, 1990, p37.).

Challenges for voluntary organisations

Strengths and weaknesses are identified by reflecting on experience. Challenges, however, require the capacity to look ahead and make preparations for the future. In this area NCVO have been particularly strong, seeing policy information as one of its most important roles. In a forward looking NCVO document 'New Times, New Challenges' Marilyn Taylor suggests that the main challenges for voluntary organisations are :

• to keep the needs of disadvantaged groups in society on the public and policy agenda;

• to continue to seek ways of exercising a constructive and effective influence on policies affecting the groups with whom we work;

- to support those who are not heard in making their needs known and becoming active on their own behalf;

- to use their experience to inform and extend debates on dependency and citizenship;

- to provide people with the information and education to make informed choices;

- to encourage active citizens to work in ways which empower those with whom they work.

These challenges find echoes in some of the major themes being addressed in this book, nearly all of which have political implications.

HISTORICAL AND POLITICAL CONTEXT

Working as a volunteer is a political act and so is running a voluntary organisation. During the 19th and 20th centuries there have been plenty of people wishing to portray volunteering and voluntary organisations as politically neutral but this is a myth. Some commentators would say that voluntary organisations have no choice but to become part of the establishment, and that the best they can achieve is to be a minor irritant in the political process.

Two examples illustrate this trend. The first, in the field of education, is the Workers Education Association. This came into being in 1903 after the failure of a number of working-class and university initiatives to do more than scratch the surface of adult education. However, its cardinal principal of being a working-class movement was undermined by the requirement to accept government money to survive, and the increasing influence of the universities.

Similarly in the field of social welfare the Charity Organisation Society, with its origins in a philanthropic reaction to the punitive Poor Laws, became an organ of selective charity rather than a political movement. William Beveridge, father of the Welfare State, saw such activity in a more positive light. He thought that 'vigour and abundance of voluntary action in association with other citizens one of the distinguishing marks of a free society' (Beveridge, Voluntary Action, quoted by Prashar, 1991).

More recent history shows there to be a very close link between organs of the state and voluntary organisations. Usha Prashar sees voluntary activity bound up with state activity since the advent of the Welfare State. 'Voluntary activity was seen as naturally evolving into statutory activity. Then it was seen as a response to bureaucratic paternalistic state welfare. Now it is seen as working in partnership with statutory authorities and others to deliver services' (Prashar, 1991).

The tendency for service-providing voluntary organisations to rely on statutory organisations for funding is symptomatic of this partnership. However beneficial such arrangements may be, and however influential the voluntary sector becomes in the development of community care, such partnerships have political dangers attached to them.

The first of these is the danger of having its strengths and creativity highjacked for purposes other than its own objectives or mission. This could pull voluntary agencies away from their roots in the community and tie them to the statutory straightjacket. A second danger is that the rhetoric of community care will not be matched by the reality of sufficient resources.

Such dangers are part of much bigger and more gradual changes in the social and political environment. Population changes and social trends, changes in the philosophy and provision of health care, attitudes to the provision of welfare, and increases in the numbers and influence of minority groups are all features of a changing environment. How the voluntary sector adapts to those changes is crucial.

SHIFTING THE BOUNDARIES OF THE WELFARE STATE

The boundaries of welfare have certainly changed since the watershed of social policy caused by the 1979 election victory of the Conservative Party. Michael McCarthy identifies a shift from state responsibility for welfare to a mixed economy or pluralist welfare system (McCarthy, 1989). He considers that the rhetoric of Conservative ideology has been more strident than the reality but feels that it has significantly influenced all areas of social policy. It has moved away from the consensus about the automatic growth and development of state welfare and has put both health care and community care at the sharp end of political debate.

Not only are these areas of social policy the subject of political debate, but they are increasingly viewed as a business to be managed rather than a service to be provided. The explicit rationale behind this is that the market is more efficient than the state. A combination of this approach plus the pluralist provision of services has led to a reduction in state responsibility and an increase in what is expected from the family, private welfare agencies and from voluntary organisations.

Such boundary shifting has important consequences for the voluntary sector. Indeed it shows up the historical dilemma, well documented during the 19th century, of voluntary organisations not only being used as organs of the status quo, but becoming institutions of repression. In more recent times it could be said that voluntary organisations have been used to cover up the inadequacies of the state.

> The ever present danger with volunteering is the use of volunteers to relieve the gross manifestations of inequality; to place a pretty counterpane over the bed with no sheets and blankets; to make just bearable the gross disadvantages that many people suffer.
>
> (Heginbotham, 1990, p35)

A key theme of this book, is that if this political cover-up is not to happen voluntary organisations have to be effectively communicating with two different sectors of society. The first of these is the *informal sector*, made up of individuals, families, communities and groups with special needs. The second is the *societal sector* of state institutions, big business and people in positions of power. The role might be thought of as one of brokerage and this idea will be developed later.

However such a role is visualised, it is clear that the voluntary sector needs to be part of the strategic planning for community care. This is emphasised in a study on implementing community care in which voluntary sector respondents argued that this should be more than the chance to comment on the planning proposals of others (Hoyes and Means, 1991, p11).

One of these respondents reported that after many years of arguing for the voluntary sector to be represented on the Joint Care Planning

Team, the decision-making body for joint planning including community care, this was eventually agreed. However, within six months a new format for decision-taking was implemented involving the chief executives of the three statutory bodies, with the voluntary sector again relegated to a consultancy role.

ROLE OF THE LOCAL AUTHORITY

Local authorities are in a difficult position given their responsibility as the main agency for developing and providing community care. Some commentators see it as being an impossible task.

> It should be clear to anyone with any sense that local authorities have been asked to perform an impossible duty: to develop care in the community with insufficient resources, a declining revenue, no ring-fenced money, and an inadequate level of managerial skill with little prospect of proper training.

> (Etherington, 1990)

The structure of local government and the changing methods of local authority finance have become notorious political footballs. The requirements of political expediency have been a nightmare for planners and for administrators with the Poll Tax saga capping it all for political opportunism. This has a direct impact on voluntary organisations, not just because of the uncertainty about funding, but because local authorities feel their role in providing community services has been continually undermined.

A further dilemma is that community care still seems to be regarded as an optional extra by some politicians. The original giants of the Welfare State, health, education, income maintenance, housing and employment, have become established as a central responsibility of society and its decision-takers. Community care, despite its equally fundamental role in maintaining a civilised and functioning population, has not yet been accepted in the same way.

A POLITICAL ROLE FOR VOLUNTARY ORGANISATIONS

It was argued earlier that voluntary organisations are inherently political. Sometimes this involves explicit action through campaigning, advocacy or some other way of exercising influence. On other occasions it is the more passive role of providing a particular service or being available as one part of the mixed economy of social welfare.

A key role, which is put forward tentatively at this stage, is that of political broker. The thinking behind this is that voluntary organisations take up a middle position between two distinct social systems. On the one hand there are *informal systems* in our society such as family, friends, neighbours, colleagues at work, shopkeepers, hairdressers and the crowd that meet at the pub on Fridays. On the other hand there are *societal systems* such as central government, local government, the Health Service, the Social Security System and the BBC which have a pervasive influence on structured social services. It is not that the informal sector cannot communicate with the societal sector or vice-versa it just needs a helping hand. A good test of political effectiveness for any voluntary organisation is to evaluate its communication skills not only with formal bodies but with individuals and community groups that require its services. Without that two-way communication the capacity to act as broker will not be possible.

Such a political balancing act would be difficult to achieve even if community care were a neat and tidy concept with evenly distributed resources. Clearly it is not, and one can find grotesque discrepancies between resources available to the informal and formal sectors, and those available to the big guns of the societal sector. A study undertaken by the Mental Health Foundation showed that six million people a year receive treatment for a medically identified mental illness. All but sixty thousand of this six million live in the community, but the bulk of funding goes to psychiatric hospitals, clearly identifiable as a societal social system. Each in-patient receives care costing £72 per day, but expenditure on the mentally ill in the community is 29p per day per person. 'It is a bit like spending the price of a four star hotel room on in-patients and the price of a cup of tea on the rest' (Mental Health Foundation, 1990).

The interesting point about those statistics is not just the figures themselves, but that the organisation which researched the subject and published data is from the voluntary sector. At the very least this kind of information has to be brought forward for political debate and perhaps form the basis for concerted action to improve resources in the community.

A further problem in promoting the role of broker is that there is still confusion within and outside voluntary organisations about what they are, what they should be doing, how they are financed and managed, and what their relationship should be with government and with statutory agencies. According to the Association of Researchers in Voluntary Action this is not a peculiarly British problem (Knapp and Kendall, 1990). It is something this book tries to address in order to make the central task of political broker a viable ambition.

SCOPE OF THE BOOK AND ITS UNDERLYING PRINCIPLES

In setting the scene for the book as a whole a number of principles are identified that exemplify the strengths of the voluntary sector and give it the authority to act as a social and political force. These principles are based on both a detached observation of the work of voluntary organisations and the hands-on experience of a decade of direct work in the field. In research terms it would probably be described as participant-observation.

1 Treating other people as equal and accepting being an equal

The concept of equality is a difficult one. We live in a hierarchical society where there are many inequalities so that attempting to run an enterprise based on equality is bound to be problematic. However, one of the base-lines for any voluntary organisation should be that there is a common level of citizenship whatever your role, position or life experience. In practice the concept is both exciting and fun. Exciting because you can sense a different kind of human communication, and fun because you can treat even the most eminent person as the same as you.

The development of this capacity to level with other people requires both positive attitudes and suitable organisational structures. For some people this is the chance they have been waiting for to express equality in their working relationships, for others it is hard work to rid themselves of the need for hierarchy. The mechanisms needed within and between organisations are partly the formal ones built in through constitutions and policy decisions, and partly the informal agreements about how to run a particular project or meeting.

2 Combining individuality with collective strength

I once heard an experienced child care worker describe the task of residential social work as providing the glue of collective support and the solvent of individuality and self-esteem. Much the same can be said of the task of voluntary organisations. Indeed Chris Heginbotham uses similar words to describe this process:

> Voluntary organisations incorporate loose networks of people, scattered throughout communities, who act as a sort of social glue. Effective use of that glue can ensure that disabled people are given their rightful place within society whilst, at the same time, their unique contributions are recognised.

(Heginbotham, 1990, p51)

Such a combination is not easily achieved, but is the essence of a philosophy which meets essential human needs within the context of a formal group.

3 Taking the lead and being responsive

Voluntary organisations have to be capable of both initiating action and responding to other people's requests and needs. Some organisations, or individuals within them, think they should always be at the forefront of new ideas, cajoling and persuading others to take up the cause or campaign which they have initiated. Others, by contrast, take the more passive view that they should only carry out what other people have asked them to do. Neither position is a satisfactory one for voluntary organisations.

A good voluntary organisation is one which can combine enthusiasm with reflection, and responsiveness with critical questioning. Both individuals and groups need to develop a degree of maturity in their functioning which does not alienate on the one hand nor come over as stodgy and sluggish on the other. To use an analogy from the theatre, one day you have to be the star and take the lead part, the next you have to be part of the supporting cast.

4 Coping with conflict

The first three principles all have contradictions implicit within them so it should be no surprise that a mini-charter of this kind makes coping with conflict one of its four key points. Conflict and contradiction are inherent in the very existence of voluntary organisations and in deciding how they should operate in a quasi-democratic society. There are several straightforward examples of this requirement.

One of these is the conflict between being an organisation which provides a service to the community while also being a critic and campaigner about such services. Another is the dilemma of having some people working in the organisation for a salary while others work in the organisation for nothing. A third example is that an organisation may at the same time try to be both an innovator and a maintainer of services. Finally there is the dilemma of wanting to be both central to the strategy of providing community care while at the same time wanting to be on the outside looking in.

These four basic principles surface at various points in the book and form part of the tussle to get to grips with the subject and to provide a coherent picture of what voluntary organisations are about. Acknowledging that there is no right way to do this it is nevertheless useful to set out how the subject will be covered in the rest of this text.

OUTLINE OF CHAPTERS

The five specific chapters which follow are designed as an examination of a particular theme and can be read as such. There are however connecting points such as the principles just outlined, so readers who select one chapter alone may miss the overall context of the book. The final chapter is a review of the major issues and an opportunity to question and challenge the future direction of voluntary organisations.

Chapter 2 is about how voluntary organisations are coping with the contract culture. This phrase may be one of the most overused in the recent history of community care, but it is of vital importance both for people within a voluntary organisation and for those whose work involves working alongside them.

Chapter 3 moves on to the topic of consumer involvement and user empowerment, an issue for the 1990s and beyond. An attempt is made to get beyond a simplistic approval of the basic ideas, and to examine different perspectives of the consumer movement and the implications for people both providing and receiving services.

Chapter 4 is devoted to the topic of voluntary organisations and the Black community. This is clearly connected to the overall theme of community acceptability but represents a contemporary challenge with wider implications for a multi-cultural society.

Chapter 5 is about partnership, principally the partnership between voluntary and statutory organisations, but also the relationship with business and the private sector. How these partnerships develop will be crucial to the future operation of voluntary organisations.

The final chapter, Chapter 6, is not quite the quest for the Holy Grail, but it is an outline of how voluntary organisations can best fulfil their role in the future. It looks at the importance of adapting to change whilst holding on to basic principles, and it suggests how the political role already referred to might be achieved. One implication is that there would have to be a change in the balance of power among political institutions as well as within voluntary organisations themselves.

REFERENCES

Ahmad B (1990) Black Perspectives in Social Work, Venture Press

Campion P *et al* (1988) 'Self-Help in Primary Care', *Journal of Royal College of General Practitioners*, October

Etherington S (1990) 'From the Front Line', *Insight*, 4 April

Heginbotham C (1990) *Return to Community*, Bedford Square Press

Hoyes L and Means R (1991) *Implementing the White Paper on Community Care*, School of Advanced Urban Studies, Bristol University

Jones K et al (1978) *Issues in Social Policy*, Routledge & Kegan Paul

Knapp M and Kendall J (1990) 'The UK Voluntary Sector in a Cross-National Context', *ARVAC Bulletin*, Winter

LGIU (1991) *The Black Community and Community Care*, Local Government Information Unit

Labour Party Consultation Document (1990) *Labour and the Voluntary Sector*

McCarthy M (1989) *The New Politics of Welfare* (Introduction) Macmillan

Mental Health Foundation (1990) *Mental Illness: the Fundamental Facts*

Prasher U (1991) 'Understanding Voluntary Action', *NCVO News*, July

Taylor M (1990) *Directions for the Next Decade*, NCVO

2
Operating in a contract culture

The contract culture is probably the biggest single challenge facing the voluntary sector in the 1990's. It raises basic questions about the role of voluntary organisations in service delivery, their independence and, in some cases, their very survival - as well as a range of complex legal, financial and other technical issues.

(National Council for Voluntary Organisations, 1990)

The term contract culture is one of a number of words or phrases dominating the social welfare and health care literature. We have got caught up in the excitement of the enterprise culture which was supposed to have regalvanised industry, and have coined our own terms to show how modern and efficient we have become.

It is possible to be wholly cynical about terms like service agreement, business plan, and quasi-market, seeing them as passing whims of academics and strategic planners. People working in the real world of running a service or organising a campaign do not need such concepts. Or do they? This chapter will explore the issue and reflect on who will benefit and who will lose from this development.

GRADUAL DEVELOPMENT OR SUDDEN DEPARTURE

Most commentators see the move to a contract culture as a developing trend rather than a new event. For some individuals and organisations it has probably come as bit of a shock, particularly if they have been so busy getting on with the job of running committees and projects that the new language and ethos has passed them by. Others think that contractual implications will not change greatly in the short term whoever is in government. They have already been around for the larger national organisations for some while and are likely to be used increasingly to finance local groups.

Ralph Kramer is even optimistic about methods of government finance, seeing the new trends as not necessarily 'corrupting, co-opting or controlling'. He suggests that most agencies have multiple sources of funds and are therefore not totally dependent on one source. He also sees the relationship between funder and provider as mutually independent, as the paying agency usually needs the services of the voluntary organisation as much as the latter requires the income. A third point he makes is that excessive monitoring, or intrusive forms of control, are unlikely as they will be too expensive to administer (Kramer, 1990a).

In another article he provides a descriptive model outlining the dominant organisational character of voluntary agencies in the UK as: charity (1970s); corporate (1980s); and contractor (1990s). This model applies primarily to larger national organisations who were the subject of his longitudinal study. For smaller local agencies the pattern is more complex.

He goes on to say that despite delays in the implementation of community care legislation there is likely to be a gradually increasing number of contracts between voluntary organisations and statutory funders. Such increases will not, however, be dramatic. We are unlikely to see either the 'dream' for large, national agencies or the 'nightmare' for smaller, local organisations (Kramer, 1990b).

It is also possible to make a distinction between 'contracting' and 'contracting out'. The former can be seen as little more than the formalisation of a process which has been going on since Social Services Departments were created twenty years ago. It may involve some expansion of services and therefore of financial support. 'Contracting out' on the other hand involves the transfer of services currently run by a local authority to another organisation. This is particularly significant in relation to residential care, but the trend brought about by the NHS and Community Care Act is likely to lead to a wide range of services being contracted out.

MISSION, MONEY AND MARKETING

These three Ms may make strange bedfellows but they are interconnected and essential elements of the management of any voluntary organisation in the field of community care. The word 'mission' seems to have gone full circle from its associations with religion and meeting the needs of the urban poor, on to an up-beat connection with business motivation and round to the aims and objectives of any voluntary organisation worth its salt.

Tim Dartington sees it as an important component of strategic planning for voluntary organisations because vaguely defined good intentions are no longer acceptable (Dartington, 1990). Some people feel it is just a way of stating the obvious, but influential American writers say that good management requires the underpinning of a mission statement. Ken Young, formerly a Director of Social Services and then Chief Executive of the Spastics Society, has spoken of the society having a mission statement 'which provided a standard against which people could make decisions throughout the organisation' (Dartington, 1990).

Mission statements based on the key values of an organisation may be important, but equally important is who decides those values and who writes a mission statement. It must be very tempting for chief executives, directors and other lead figures in a voluntary organisation to see this as their role. However, if this mission statement is to be understood and followed it has to be owned by those people directly involved in the service, project or campaign. The most a chief executive should be in this respect is therefore an enabler.

One danger of mission statements is that they narrow aims and objectives down to those which fit a particular service or the views of a funding body. There is then the possibility that voluntary organisations would just become agents of the state. The concern to some people is that energy would be concentrated on providing acceptable services, to the neglect of political influence, advocacy and campaigning.

The connection between this concern and money is very clear. Money talks. It is not necessarily a dirty word, but it certainly dictates both the quantity and quality of the service provided. In his study of twenty national charities Kramer shows that overall income increased from £36.5 million in 1976 to £63.3 million in 1987, which implies an annual average increase of 6 per cent over inflation. (Kramer, 1990b) This seems to be the pattern for voluntary organisations providing a service which statutory organisations wish to support.

21

The figures are sometimes more dramatic in small, local agencies. In 1976, the first year of Kramer's study, Oxford MIND, a small local voluntary organisation, had an income of £860; by 1987 it had gone up to £80,000. In 1990 the organisation negotiated its first service agreement with Oxfordshire County Council, a procedure much more long-winded than the previous applications for grant aid. The result was a long-term commitment to two established day centres, a new sum towards the employment of a director and a firmer set of expectations about the role of a voluntary organisation in the provision of community care.

One concern is that contractual funding for particular services focuses attention on the unit price of a service rather than also acknowledging the need of organisation for core funding. As Stuart Etherington so graphically states, 'markets are all the rage in social welfare' (Etherington, 1990). It is one of those in-words developed to a nicety by Le Grand and colleague at Bristol where the more developed term is 'quasi-markets' (Le Grand, 1990). Etherington is more down-to-earth in creating a distinction between industrial and consumer markets. He suggests that ideas from industrial marketing are more useful for voluntary organisations than those from consumer markets. In one sense he is right as one is not selling ties or going bust when the market for fancy socks dries up. Industrial marketing helps to distinguish different roles in the process of making agreements or drawing up contracts. There are the users and potential users of a service, those who approve the decision, and those who act as gatekeepers at any stage of this process. Each of these has to be influenced and marketing has to be relevant and understandable.

Kramer sees this process as changing the relationship with local government 'from supplicant-patron to supplier-purchaser; from asking for support or generosity to negotiating deals' (Kramer, 1990a). In many ways it is a healthier relationship based on a more equal partnership. Kramer considers the metaphor of a market more appropriate than the concept of partnership. He sees this market structured by four sets of conditions:

i)   The *demand* for contracting as seen through legislation, government policy, precedents, and practical considerations such as the availability of services at a reasonable price.

ii)   The *supply* of potential providers of services which are
      required and the existence of enough buyers or a big enough
      buyer to make the marketing worthwhile.

iii) The *character of the service product*, whether it is tangible
      (e.g. meals), measurable (e.g. numbers and effectiveness in
      a day centre), and capable of costing (e.g. amount per bed).

iv)   The *socio-political context* including the history of relations
      between voluntary organisations and statutory bodies in any
      community, local political concerns, special interests of
      senior administrators, and the informal networks of a
      particular locality or interest group.

                                        (Kramer and Grossman, 1987)

The overall message about marketing for voluntary organisations is
that it requires understanding of the nature of the market,
acknowledgement of the different levels and role of the buyers, and
the patience to work out a contract which is agreeable to the funding
source and acceptable within the agency.

THE NATIONAL–LOCAL DIVIDE

As referred to earlier one scenario portrayed for this new era is that
what would be a dream for national bodies would become a nightmare
for local organisations. Local voluntary agencies have become doubly
dependent in their search for secure funds, first on the policies of
central government, and second on the policies of local government,
themselves victims of centralised control. Kramer describes this as 'an
extended, dramatic struggle for power between central and local
government in which voluntary organisations are caught in the middle
– with the larger national agencies seemingly beneficiaries – and local,
community based organisations as likely losers' (Kramer, 1990b).

   Local authorities have become the designated lead agency for
community care yet there is little confidence that they will have either
the required resources or the political support from central government
to make it work. Richard Gutch at NCVO sees a whole series of
changes involving the roles of both local government and voluntary
organisations. He suggests that it is not a question of rivalry between
local government and the voluntary sector but rather the danger of

23

becoming simply agents and thus losing their own identities. 'Local government is in danger of becoming the agent of central government, implementing policies determined in Whitehall. The voluntary sector is in danger of becoming the agent of local government, functioning more like a department of the local authority than an independent organisation' (Gutch, 1990).

Kramer links this directly to restrictions on local authority spending and to the means for raising revenue at their disposal. With limited tax powers and financial disincentives for direct service provision, voluntary agencies are entering agreements with a financially weak enabler-partner (Kramer, 1990b).

In this aura of gloom it has to be remembered that not only have the incomes of voluntary organisations increased continually over the last fifteen years, but they are not generally dependent on only one source of funds. The annual reports of the voluntary organisation referred to earlier show that although nearly 50 per cent of its income comes from the local authority, substantial funds also come from Joint Finance, the Health Authority, a Charitable Trust, its Charity Shop, income from investments and a long list of individual and corporate donors (Oxford MIND Annual Reports, 1988–90).

IMPACT ON NEW, SMALL, AND MINORITY-INTEREST ORGANISATIONS

In a legendary quip on a golf course, Sammy Davis Junior is said to have been asked 'Hey, Sammy, what's your handicap?' He replied, 'I'm a one-eyed Jewish Negro, what's yours?' Certain small voluntary organisations and self-help groups must feel like responding in the same way, but without the style and charisma of Sammy Davis. In a similar way Ken Livingstone's book *If Voting Changed Anything They'd Abolish It* reflects in the title the frustration of being out in the cold as an anti-establishment figure. Many voluntary organisations found that they too were out in the cold when the Greater London Council was abolished.

One of the concerns of some voluntary organisations in the current atmosphere is that they will be viewed by funding bodies as too small, too way-out or too concerned with a minority interest. Even an organisation as established as Age Concern argues strongly that contracts should not be used to replace grants. They should not be seen as a terrible threat nor as a magic wand, but local Age Concern groups are warned not to be conned by the image or importance which such contracts imply. (Age Concern, 1990)

Marilyn Taylor argues that the benefits of the new funding arrangements are nearly all with the bigger, more established agencies. She thinks that public authorities are likely to prefer one large contract to a plethora of smaller ones, and even when small organisations are successful they will take on the features of larger agencies (Taylor, 1990). She thinks it is possible to see a more optimistic scenario with a variety of services under the aegis of 'a truly enabling authority'. In such a scenario individuals could become partners in developing and providing services, 'shaping overall patterns of provision as well as influencing their own care packages'. Such a possibility is only likely with a different kind of local democracy from that available at present. It would require vision, political courage and release from past prejudices, not to mention the re-thinking of the agency mentality described by Gutch.

Black voluntary organisations and community groups may be particularly vulnerable in this respect. Adrian Williams says 'It is arguable whether or not there are more than a handful of Black organisations in London which are equipped to enter into contracts. There are at an educated guess, even fewer that know what is entailed in a contract' (Williams, 1990).

Ivan Hendry in writing about experience in Birmingham is even more alarmed at the overall scene.

> The greatest threat that the Contract Culture poses is that small new voluntary organisations will be starved of funds and the traditional source of ideas for meeting new needs will dry up. In effect the well-springs of social innovation will be blocked. This would be a great loss for society in general. For specific communities with distinct cultural needs it will mean increased marginalisation and alienation.

> (Hendry, 1990)

The occasional Black community group tackles this trend on its own terms. Stonebridge is described in an NCVO Information Pack produced in 1990 as 'a typical run-down inner city, high rise estate of some 20,000 people with the largest black population ratio in the United Kingdom and Europe – 70% Afro-Caribbean, 20% Asian.' The Harlesden People's Community Council outline their transition from a spontaneous group to a bureaucracy and then on to an enterprise where the language of 'business, profit and share-holding' is acceptable.

This project seems atypical both in its approach to providing community services and in its relationship to a funding borough. It does however demonstrate that a community council in a deprived area can find people with entrepreneurial skills and the will to meet fund providers as equal partners.

THE LOCAL AUTHORITY PERSPECTIVE

As many local voluntary organisations have found, the attitude of key personnel in their local authority is vital in the process of negotiating contracts and service agreements. Understanding of how the voluntary sector operates, the development of trust between negotiators, and a willingness to give sufficient time to the discussions are all important elements of this process.

Keith Hawley, who was the main negotiator with voluntary organisations in Oxfordshire described his role as changing from 'Community Development Worker' to 'Contract Manager'. This gave his job more focus rather than changing the basic task and he saw the contracting approach as less significant than the overall political priorities and financial capabilities of local government. In this respect he echoed the views of Gutch and Kramer.

There are two limitations in what can be achieved. First, a service seen as essential by a voluntary organisation may be viewed as optional by a local authority under financial pressure. Second if the pot of money available in the form of grants is drastically reduced there is limited scope for new initiatives. On the other hand, Community Care legislation and money offers new ways of providing services and encourages local authorities to look to voluntary, not-for-profit, and private agencies to bring these about.

In contrast to some authorities Oxfordshire has been making service agreements with both providers of a direct service, and support organisations such as the Council for Voluntary Action and Age Concern, Oxfordshire. It is also willing in principle to support the needs of newer minority groups and has helped to fund a West Indian Day Centre, Oxaids and Body Positive. Groups which fit a local authority's own priorities and complement its own Social Services department are probably in the best position to be supported. Some will be more financially secure than projects run by the department itself, none of which have a contract to turn to when the going gets tough.

For local authorities the going seems to be getting tougher all the time. One of the root causes is the inability of government to find a politically acceptable source of local authority finance. The two main parties shy away from local income tax, thus leading to unsatisfactory systems like the community charge or a charge based on property.

The impact on voluntary organisations during periods of political angst and financial conflict is often hidden. The London Voluntary Service Council estimated that for 1991 the London voluntary sector would lose at least £15 million, and outside London cuts of a further £15 million were predicted in a range of different areas including Manchester, Newcastle, Derbyshire, Bournemouth, Basingstoke and Avon (NCVO, 1991). Such cuts contradict stated government policy and are a frustration to both the voluntary sector and local authorities which wish to support them. NCVO sees such cuts falling particularly heavily on local development agencies, advice agencies and training programmes, all essential elements in any programme for increasing the contribution of the voluntary sector to community care.

A WIDER VIEW

So far this chapter has taken a narrow view of the idea of contracts and has located the discussion entirely in Britain. The American experience of giving more responsibility to both voluntary and private agencies has led to problems of 'vendorism, grantmanship and dependency' (Kramer, 1981). In his later writing he reflects that contracts are distinguished in the USA by tighter, more explicit and more rigorous criteria for funding. 'Contracting requires greater specificity of objectives and a credible capacity to achieve particular service outcomes in a cost effective and accountable way' (Kramer, February 1990a).

Such activities may be worthwhile if voluntary organisations become more clear thinking, provide a more focused service and gain in confidence as partners in the provision of community care. The American experience, however, offers warning signs that should not be ignored. The widening gap between privilege and poverty cannot be bridged by voluntary agencies, neither can they make up the shortfall in a federal budget deficit. Voluntary agencies may be able to respond creatively to 'the mosaic society' described by Geneva Johnson, but not if their income is restricted to providing services of which a reactionary government approves. Her response is to acknowledge the entrepreneurial and competitive system and provide voluntary organisations with better leadership and the capacity to handle systematised information and efficient negotiations:

> Service providers will have to respond competitively to the new environment or they will cease to exist. Government will continue to play a significant, but reduced, direct service role which will continue to be reflected through purchase of service mechanisms and limited to a permanent welfare class.

(Johnson, 1990)

Such a vision is not attractive to voluntary organisations who see themselves as providing a service to the whole community and who hope to help to reduce social inequalities not to exacerbate them. Two writers have argued that the voluntary sector should be in the forefront of changing the current political emphasis not just reacting to the current trends. Chris Heginbotham says that 'the voluntary sector has a major, if not crucial, role to play in building a new communitarian approach' (Heginbotham, 1990). This echoes the views of Paul Hoggett who writes, 'The conditions now exist for a new form of collectivism, one in which strong and confident local state institutions enter into a form of social contract with the myriad organisations of civil society' (Hoggett, 1990).

The latter's vision is not shared by many working in the field but Hoggett's optimism and willingness to bring the idea of a *social* contract back into discussion is encouraging for those who see voluntary organisations as a political force and not merely service providers for a struggling society.

TOWARDS A CODE OF PRACTICE

Is it possible for voluntary organisations to have some formal guidance about how to handle this new era of contracts and service agreements? The National Council for Voluntary Organisations believes that it is. In seeking the views of individuals and organisations throughout the country the council has begun developing a code of practice based on underlying principles which it considers essential for the provision of good services.

These principles form a continuum which makes the views and involvement of service users a high priority, emphasises the importance of quality, variety and choice, highlights the importance of involving voluntary sector Black and other ethnic minority groups, and implies a free and open discussion between the statutory purchasers and the voluntary sector providers (NCVO, 1990).

The Code of Guidance arising from these discussions makes additional emphasis on recognising the needs of carers and on safeguarding the independence of voluntary organisations. It addresses practice implications to local and national voluntary organisations which provide direct services as well as to umbrella bodies, development agencies and statutory agencies (NCVO, 1991).

It is important that such codes of practice are not too complicated and detailed as there is a danger that they will then become a dead-weight on negotiating parties rather than the support and help intended. A key message is to operate through negotiation rather than competition, something many local authorities would welcome hearing from government as well as from the voluntary sector. Perhaps the most useful feature of such guidelines is to provide principles which statutory agencies would work to in negotiating financial support for voluntary groups. A specific suggestion in the draft code is that 'there should be a spectrum of different kinds of funding agreement, which would include *grants* for organisations just starting up and for projects involving community development, advocacy or innovation; *service agreements* for organisations whose work can be expressed in terms of general outputs but where a degree of flexibility is required; and *detailed contracts* for services which can be defined purely in terms of specific outputs' (NCVO, 1990).

CONCLUSIONS

One dispiriting conclusion is that it is very difficult for voluntary organisations to take the lead, either in the political sense or in how funding arrangements should develop. Voluntary organisations have become well-meaning sheep, dependent on the nature of both the local sheep dog and the national shepherd. Despite the preference of British society for the status quo a kind of restructuring has been taking place which is permeating through from industrial and technological changes. One view is that the Conservative strategy of the last decade has introduced market rationality into an over-bureaucratised welfare state. The gradual break-up of state provision and the coming together of pluralised welfare automatically changes the role played by voluntary organisations. The contract culture is a feature of this change.

There seems no choice for voluntary organisations but to react to such restructuring. Societies with democratic and capitalist traditions tend to make social and political reforms which reflect industrial, commercial and technological changes. Politicians and social reformers sometimes talk as if it is the other way round but this only happens rarely. Russia in the 1920s or Cuba in the 1950s come to mind – neither good examples of a democratic tradition nor of a healthy voluntary sector.

The role of local government has become crucial to the financing of voluntary organisations both because of its traditional support through grant-aid and because it has been handed the responsibility for community care. Unfortunately the development of community care schemes is a lower political priority than reducing the amount that citizens are required to pay through rates, poll tax, council tax or whatever alternative system is devised. The saga and political fiasco of local government finance is unlikely to be resolved speedily and this will reinforce the uncertainty experienced by many small voluntary organisations.

One outcome of recent changes has been to focus attention on the different funding alternatives available to the voluntary sector. The guidelines produced by NCVO have highlighted what kind of funding arrangement is best suited to the various projects and services which are being run or newly developed. Although some commentators have expressed concern that national and established projects will benefit at the expense of local and undeveloped schemes, others see there being an overall benefit in the new approach. The importance of not becoming dependent on one funding source is now clearly established.

A further point to emerge in examining this theme is how easy it would be for some voluntary organisations to take on more than they should. A fine balance has to be struck between being an initiator and service developer on the one hand and becoming the total provider and service dustbin for a particular client group. Some statutory bodies would be only too happy to shift both blame and responsibility on to unsuspecting voluntary groups. It will be important to be neither beguiled nor bemused by the attraction of status and security which some contracts offer. As some American projects have shown, this can lead to loss of identity, a blunted critical edge, and an increase in social control.

One important question to ask when discussing the contract culture, is what impact is it having on the consumers of services. Kramer suggests that 'there is virtually no information on what difference it makes to users of social service if it is under one auspice or another' (Kramer, 1990a). This is somewhat disturbing if one looks to voluntary agencies as the best placed to be responsive to consumers. Exploring the significance of user participation and empowerment will be the focus of the next chapter.

REFERENCES

Age Concern (1990) *Contracts and the Contract Culture: An Introductory Guide for Age Concern Groups*

Dartington T (1990) 'New Words for New Times', *NCVO News* December

Etherington S (1990) 'From the Front Line', *Insight*, 14 March

Gutch R (1990) 'Partners or Agents?' *NCVO Community Care Newsletter* December

Heginbotham C (1990) *Return to Community*, Bedford Square Press: p41

Hendry I (1990) *Contracts for Care*, NCVO Information Pack for Black and other Ethnic Minority Groups, September

Hoggett P (1990) *Modernisation, Political Strategy and the Welfare State*, University of Bristol (SAUS), July: p52

Johnson G (1990) 'The Need for Leadership', *NCVO News*, December

Kramer R (1981) *Voluntary Agencies in the Welfare State*, University of California Press, 1981

Kramer R and Grossman B (1987) 'Contracting for Social Services', *Social Services Review* No. 61

Kramer R (1990a) *Voluntary Organisations in the Welfare State: On The Threshold of the '90s*, The Centre for Voluntary Organisations, Paper 8, February

—— (1990b) 'Change and Continuity in British Voluntary Organisations 1976 to 1988', *International Journal of Voluntary and Non-Profit Organisations (Voluntas)*, Vol.1, No. 2

Le Grand J (1990) *Quasi-Markets and Social Policy*, University of Bristol (SAUS)

Livingston, K (1988) *If Voting Changed Anything They'd Abolish It*, Fontana

NCVO (1990) News Bulletin – Contract Culture Supplement, December

—— (1991) *Briefing Paper on Contracting*, NCVO, March

Taylor M (1990) 'Change Partners Please', *Social Work Today*, 18 October

Williams A (1990) 'Contract Friendly or Contract Deadly?' *NCVO Community Care Newsletter*, December

3
Consumer involvement and user empowerment

'Survivors of the system are no more consumers of services than cockroaches are consumers of Rentokil.'

(Campaign Against Psychiatric Oppression)

Deciding on the title for this chapter has required considerable thought. The words themselves and how they are perceived are very important and it is freely acknowledge that they will not suit all readers. Indeed some voluntary organisations explicitly reject the terms consumer and user: 'The survivors are not consumers (there is little or no choice), and not service users which would imply an unnecessary level of dependence' (George, 1991). Despite such reservations these words seem the best available at present. It is certainly a vital issue for voluntary organisations and perhaps the biggest challenge to their right to exist. In exploring this theme there is an underlying assumption and explicit belief that all voluntary organisations should involve consumers to some degree.

The chapter will start by examining the principles and philosophy which any voluntary organisation needs to have explored in the process of deciding on its mission. It will then look at the potential for consumer involvement both nationally and locally with particular emphasis on organisations for minority groups, ethnic communities and citizen advocacy. A crucial topic is the relationship between consumers and workers in any organisation and whether they support and empower each other. The conclusion will address some of the political issues and the role of voluntary organisations as sources of influence in statutory community care services.

PHILOSOPHY, PRINCIPLES AND OTHER IMPORTANT WORDS

It is relatively easy to find positive words such as autonomy, participation, involvement and empowerment and also possible to evoke negative concepts such as being ignored, discarded and oppressed. It is much more difficult to establish what these words mean in practice and how to make positive principles operational. There are paradoxes and ironies in abundance. Mike Lawson experienced being more 'used' than being a user, yet also recalls the sense of identity and relief he felt when being told 'you are a schizophrenic'. This was hard for him to imagine later when becoming a leading figure in both MIND and in Survivors Speak Out as he recognised what mental-health language had done to him and other psychiatric patients (Lawson, 1988).

Whether in recognising one's oppression or discovering one's potential for autonomy, many individuals have used voluntary organisations as a vehicle for this process. Originally this seems to have happened more by accident than design. The 1980s, however, saw a dramatic growth in voluntary organisations which deliberately sought the views of consumers. For some people this can only be done by setting up organisations which are exclusively for consumers and are run by that group of people. Other organisations have space for 'allies' so long as they accept a secondary role. More traditional agencies have tried to increase consumer involvement without encouraging consumer take-over. Judi Chamberlin has usefully designated these different types of organisation as *separatist*, *supportive* and *partnership* models (Chamberlin, 1988). Whichever model is adopted, any movement forward is likely to involve an element of conflict.

Few people within the voluntary sector will find difficulty in the idea that consumers should have a say about their own lives and whether or not they find a particular service helpful. What is more problematic is whether they should take decisions about how services are run, who staffs them and who should hold the money. In a neatly titled report 'From Paternalism to Participation', Suzy Croft and Peter Beresford point out the importance of being clear about this. People need to know whether they are being offered more control over the services they receive as individuals, or whether they are being asked to take some responsibility for the management, planning and development of a particular service or organisation (Croft and Beresford, 1990).

Writers as diverse as Chris Heginbotham and Paulo Freire see a link between breaking away from personal and professional oppression through participation and consumerism to a more powerful position of citizenship and 'conscientization'. Heginbotham sees it as part of a return to a communitarian ideal and away from the worst excesses of individualism (Heginbotham, 1990). Freire's perspective is more overtly political being based in the oppression of South America. Education is seen as a liberating and empowering experience where the aim is not to fill empty minds, but to release potential through dialogue, shared experiences, and a belief in the power to change structures (Freire, 1972).

Empowerment is a difficult but crucial concept for the social welfare field to address. Two questions need to be asked: why is empowerment considered desirable and what does it mean in practice? To take the 'why' question first. First, if personal or group empowerment can be achieved among people who are relatively powerless it can have a significant effect both on their physical and mental health and on their attitude towards powerful people and institutions. 'The process of achieving those goals involves an improvement in people's image of themselves, the acquisition of tangible resources such as money or shelter and intangible resources such as information and the creation of supportive social networks' (Rees, 1991).

A second reason why empowerment is an important concept is that it offers a way for acting on underlying political and economic issues. Although economic rationalism and individualism has been the dominant political ethic in the 1980s, the axis of political debate could well be tilted towards social justice again through the energy of politically aware individuals and groups – voluntary organisations among them.

What does empowerment mean in practice and what models can be used to help voluntary organisations understand how to go about it? First there is the task of discovering sources of power, influence and authority. Fromm suggests that authority can be external, internal or anonymous (Fromm, 1960). Voluntary bodies might find it more useful to widen those sources and see them as personal, professional, organisational and political. This implies seeking sources of power within ourselves, our organisations and the political structure.

Rees points out an interesting model and source of ideas for developing empowerment, both personal and political. This is the women's movement. Feminist perspectives have helped to identify sources of victimisation and the location of problems in male-dominated traditions, institutions and attitudes. This has in turn led to social, economic and legal reforms, often using networks of support among women and alternative social services based on feminist values (Rees, 1991).

Voluntary organisations have the potential both for educating and liberating people who may become stuck in roles, whether as client, patient, worker or manager. They can also be a means for developing the skills necessary to run things, take decisions and cope with responsibility. Exercising power is a skilful process.

Key issues which voluntary organisations need to address and clarify are the level of involvement and participation of service users, the implications of empowerment for change in the organisation, and the support that can be given to newly emerging consumer-led groups.

OPERATING AT DIFFERENT LEVELS AND IN DIFFERENT WAYS

The level of involvement and the degree of empowerment brought about by that involvement are important areas of consideration whether operating locally, regionally, nationally or internationally. This section particularly examines the local scene but also takes account of how voluntary organisations operate nationally.

A starting-point is at the level of the individual. Many commentators stress that 'it should be the individual users who decides what treatment or care he or she receives' (Bowden, 1988). This is easier said than done and requires thought and persistence to put into practice. A good example of giving control to users can be found in the London Borough of Croydon. The scheme for recruiting carers for people with a severe physical disability is based round the individual interviewing and appointing their own paid carers. This involves a training course in how to select staff, learning how to draw up a job description, and working out how to plan, conduct and evaluate a selection interview (Ogden, 1991).

Small projects in the community, whether providing residential, day care or other services, should be offering a minimum level of involvement to their customers. In order to bring this about the following four approaches can be used:

1 **A regular forum open to all current users of a service which can discuss day-to-day issues or problems.** This is more effective if chaired or co-ordinated by a service user but does not necessarily involve a formal election. The forum needs to be clearly advertised and held at a regular time and may have some time with staff present and other time with only users present.

2 **Direct involvement in key operational decisions such as staff appointments and new residents.** Some small projects can involve anybody who wants to be included in such a process while others choose or elect people for a particular task. Staff appointments are particularly important for any community project and the sense of commitment to a particular worker can be greatly enhanced by including users in the selection process. It is important for applicants to know the basis of the selection procedure including where the power to make the ultimate decisions resides. Such ways of operating take far more time than a standard interview but it is usually found to be time well spent.

3 **Users being on formal committees of a voluntary organisation.** This is happening more and more with a number of voluntary organisations having a constitutional requirement that users are on management committees. The pattern of such meetings probably needs to change from the formal sitting round a table for a fixed length of time to something more varied and enjoyable. One organisation in the mental health field does most of its business in small huddles which then report decisions to the whole committee. This also includes a 'pizza break' which is more sustaining than a coffee break.

4 **Use of workshops and other devices for increasing communication and involvement.** These are particularly good for taking stock of long term plans, deciding on mission

statements, and agreeing policy on strategic issues. In running such events it is worth remembering that the location needs to be accessible and friendly, you probably need two or more facilitators, and proceedings go better if food and drink are readily available. Some people need to be told what a 'workshop' is. The professionals and experienced users often take this for granted but if your working life has been spent in steel-making or you have spent time in prison then 'workshop' is thought of in other ways.

So far this sounds friendly and co-operative, both hallmarks of sensitive and supportive voluntary organisations. However, some new voluntary organisations have felt it necessary to take a much more strident and less co-operative stance. In *The Case for Separation* Judi Chamberlin makes a strongly worded case for ex-patient groups and other mental health user groups to be totally separate from organisations which include professionals or non-patients (Chamberlin, 1987). She sees the key tasks of such groups as:

(a) Consciousness raising (modelled on the experience of Black, women's and gay groups).

(b) Changing mental health terminology by challenging 'mentalism' and 'sane chauvinism'.

(c) Changing attitudes which have limited opportunities for psychiatric patients.

(d) Allowing the legitimate expression of anger towards the system.

Various means can be used to carry out these tasks. She suggests support groups, advocacy schemes, public speaking, newsletters (such as *Madness Network News*), artistic activities, and providing alternative services. It is interesting that in practice the organisations which have evolved from this philosophy in America have split into those working with the mental health system and those which insist on staying outside. It is clearly very difficult to have an effective voice, let alone any power, if an organisation insists on staying outside the welfare system.

An example of a voluntary organisation which has taken the middle road of being primarily for users but accepting non-user 'allies' as members is Survivors Speak Out. This would fall into the category described by Chamberlin as supportive rather than separatist. It is interesting that within five years it has established itself at local, national and international levels with an impressive leadership, the capacity to publish articles and papers, and a reputation for strong but sensible views about both old and new services.

Perhaps the best example in the same field of a partnership model is MIND which operates nationally, regionally and through local organisations. MIND has changed its ethos and its constitution to become a partnership of users, concerned individuals and mental health professionals. This has not been without struggle or conflict, but the discomfort for some has meant new and positive involvement for others. Standing still is not an option for creative and effective voluntary organisations.

VOLUNTARY GROUPS FROM ETHNIC COMMUNITIES

The need for effective user involvement is particularly important when services are being provided for minority groups. Bandana Ahmad suggests that the philosophy of empowerment has far reaching implications because of the oppression experienced by Black people. She therefore considers it inadequate to acknowledge the various disadvantages suffered by Black people (e.g. poverty, poor housing, unemployment, ill health), unless steps are taken by workers and organisations to tackle the racism which pervades all areas of community care. This implies giving Black communities and individual workers the responsibility and the resources to develop and run their own services (Ahmad, 1990).

For the voluntary sector two parallel approaches need to be taken to ensure positive action. Existing services need to take account of their local ethnic communities through various forms of communication. This may take the form of formal consultation with community leaders and current users of services or be approached less predictably using community events, student projects, religious meetings and publications in relevant languages.

The parallel method does not involve integration into current services, but the setting up of separate and distinct groups and organisations. Such services should have a number of advantages:

(a) With direct access and a clear Black identity they should avoid the negative filter of using standard referral systems.

(b) There should be no significant division between users, carers and workers. The barriers which can exist are likely to be less significant because the racial identity element will be a stronger influence.

(c) Any organisation which is successful in meeting people's needs and solving personal problems will become a source of community pride.

(d) The group or organisation can become a basis for campaigning, community education and participation in planning.

As well as service providing and campaigning groups at local level there is also the need for umbrella organisations which take a broader view and provide expertise across a wider geographical area. Such an organisation is the Standing Conference of Ethnic Minority Senior Citizens. This provides a development role, offers advocacy services, and is able to represent the views of minority communities to local and national government (George, 1991).

ADVOCACY SERVICES

It can be argued that in an era where community care has become big business for statutory, private and voluntary organisations the need for independent advocacy for people who are vulnerable and have weak voices is more important than ever. But what is advocacy, what does it involve and how should the voluntary sector respond to this issue? Clearly it involves providing advice and information, dealing with welfare rights, and undertaking some kind of representation. The key element which directs each of these tasks is the view of the consumers themselves. Thus in psychiatric services in Holland the advocate's task is 'to defend the interests of the patient as the patient himself defines them' (Robson, 1987).

Several types or models of advocacy can be described, all of which can be linked to voluntary organisations. These are: paid advocacy; citizens advocacy; self advocacy; service brokerage.

Paid advocacy

This is probably best known in the form of legal advocacy with examples in some large psychiatric hospitals. Projects which started with a legal purpose have frequently moved on to include broader welfare rights issues, and more recently to take an active part in the transition from long-stay hospitals to smaller community residential schemes.

Citizens advocacy

The key element in this approach is the use of ordinary citizens as skilled volunteers, supported by an independent agency. Like paid advocacy, some good examples can be found in the field of learning disability, often providing long-term support and a continuing voice for people with profound difficulties. Some legislation, such as the Disabled Person's (Services, Consultation, Representation) Act 1986, has supported these initiatives but as a way of thinking and in its operation it is still in its infancy.

Self advocacy

This is central to the whole philosophy of consumer empowerment and client-centred planning and decision-making. Self advocacy means people speaking and acting for themselves. It acknowledges that certain clients and patients are easily marginalised by professionals. It involves gaining access to information and being informed, because without adequate information it is not possible to make real choices.

Service brokerage

Although developed particularly in Canada since the mid-1970s, the idea of service brokerage is relatively new in Britain. David Brandon, from his base in Preston, Lancashire, has developed and written about a scheme based on the right of individuals to plan their own life, who may require some support to do this effectively. It is more radical than some other approaches because it requires the funding body to hand over financial entitlement direct to the consumer. From this point the broker acts like a travel agent to gather information, explain the options and negotiate the purchase of services. One of the fascinating aspects of the scheme so far is that the services purchased have tended to come from the informal or voluntary sector not statutory services (Brandon, 1991).

41

A role for voluntary organisations can be found in each of these models. With the paid advocacy scheme large institutions have found that setting up small independent bodies is both more acceptable and more effective than trying to run schemes themselves. Citizens advocacy was pioneered by groups like Advocacy Alliance, a consortium of national voluntary organisations (MENCAP, One to One, The Spastics Society, MIND and the Leonard Cheshire Foundation). Local schemes will invariably be led by and co-ordinated by voluntary organisations or umbrella groups such as councils for voluntary action. Self advocacy schemes also need the support and expertise which a competent voluntary agency can provide. An interesting project in Nottingham offers all three forms of advocacy under the title Nottingham Advocacy Group. The service brokerage scheme in Lancashire is co-ordinated by the Service Brokerage Board, 'a voluntary organisation composed of about a dozen members who are, hopefully, a good cross-section of the community' (Brandon,1991).

Although the voluntary sector clearly has an important role to play in the development and management of different advocacy schemes, some dangers can be seen. For example, the kind of organisation needed may not attract funds from statutory bodies, particularly those which have rigid views about service contracts or are short of money. A Citizens Charter and formal complaints procedures will not be enough to ensure a voice for those citizens who have a long-term requirement for community care or whose short-term needs are for very specific services. Advocacy schemes need considerable support to get started and, once the service is known, to function adequately. As Marilyn Taylor says: 'They depend on a well-developed network of intermediary and development agencies, which provide the information, training and support which allows them to survive on very limited funding. This voluntary sector infrastructure is no longer likely to be at a premium in a market oriented to front-line services' (Taylor, 1992).

BALANCING THE NEEDS OF CONSUMERS AND WORKERS

Achieving more power as a consumer is not a neutral experience. It affects the people directly concerned and it also affects those with whom they have a significant relationship. In particular it affects the relationship between the user of a community service and those who are employed to run it. This relationship is not a simple one and can be both complex and variable, particularly at times of change.

In voluntary organisations which provide a direct community service the work-force, both paid and volunteer, is the primary resource and most valuable asset. The organisation as a whole, as well as increasingly involved users, needs to take account of this if the progress made on consumer empowerment is not to lead to alienation of the workforce. Workers are frequently in the frontline pushing for greater user participation but even when there is a shared goal in this respect there can be difficulties. If workers are not sympathetic to changes or to the methods being used to achieve change a recipe for conflict and possible disaster can be created. In such a scenario workers become defensive and resistant to change, and users become dictatorial and unsympathetic.

The aim must therefore be to empower consumers of services without undermining workers' professional and personal capacity to do the job well. Mutual empowerment is the desirable goal but considerable thought has to be given to the process of achieving it. In several respects voluntary organisations have a head-start over statutory bodies in seeking to achieve such a goal. Their mission and even their constitution may point them in this direction, their scale of operation may enable personal relationships to flourish more easily, and the type of person who seeks employment in the voluntary sector may be more responsive to the philosophy of consumer empowerment.

Thinking through the implications of increasing user involvement is important for both workers and users. The new roles required of both parties may create tension and are bound to be challenging. 'To the professional staff it is challenging because of a perceived loss of power. To the service user it is challenging because it demands greater responsibility both for one's own life, but also for articulating the support needed within the community and taking appropriate steps to ensure that that support is provided' (Bowden, 1988).

Even those who are particularly positive about increasing user involvement are liable to discomfort and uncertainty. This applies to users as well as workers. Thinking it through is likely to involve conflict and the process of returning power to consumers is bound to be hard work. One worker looking back over three years with a community project described the process as 'difficult, isolated and stressful, but often encouraging, positive and hopeful too' (Harvey, 1987). She found that on some occasions it was best for workers and users to work separately and on other occasions more effective to work together.

If having more control over your own life and the services you need to enhance that control is to be achieved, users have to find common ground with workers. Employees and volunteers can also be victimised and oppressed. An association with Paulo Freire's ideas has been made earlier in this chapter, but they are particularly appropriate in this context. Education as the means of liberation dominates Freire's thinking, but it involves the teacher learning with the student. In the same way the worker has to learn alongside the user:

> Workers must no longer perceive their role as offering palliatives to the sick, they must engage with users in a process of empowerment. They must recognise that they bring with them their prejudices and their deformations, which include a lack of confidence in people's ability to think, to want and to know.

> (Barker & Peck, 1987)

It is important to accept that workers can be a hindrance to user involvement either consciously or without knowing it. Lawson uses strong language to make the point:

> workers who maintain the old myths and give lip-service to advocacy and self-determination are as much a hindrance as the prescription and electric shock merchants who just add to the vast coffers of the multi-national pharmaceutical companies and damage the body and brain.

> (Lawson, 1988)

In a similar way it should be recognised that consumers can be a hindrance to their own empowerment. The reluctance to move from dependency on staff is well recognised whether in the big decisions of life or day-to-day activities.

> 'Nurse, will you make me a cup of tea?'
> 'No, Peter, my name's Kate and I will have a cup of tea with you, if you put the kettle on.'

> (Harvey, 1987)

This simple dialogue gives some clues about the nature of the change which has to take place if workers give up power and users accept it. There has to be open communication on an equal level. If first names are used they should be used by everybody. There should be none of the classic interchange so familiar in hospitals.

'Hello, Lil. How are you today?'

'Very well, thank you doctor.'

Whatever the setting it should enable workers and users to bring their natural, less formal attributes into play rather than being tied to formal roles of client, patient, member of staff, volunteer or manager. This in itself can be a liberating experience because it does not deny the formal roles but allows them to develop more creatively. This section concludes with two key questions and some incomplete answers.

Question 1

If you walk into a day centre, therapeutic community or any community-based project can you tell who are the staff and who are the users? If you cannot tell the difference does that worry you?

The first question is a challenge to the project itself. There should be no obvious distinction between workers and users who should convey a sense of belonging, a sense of ownership and a sense of openness to the outside world.

The second question is a challenge to the visitor. Some people feel uncomfortable if they cannot discern who is in charge or who is needing treatment. It is not just the workers and users who have to adjust to a different ethos, people from the outside world have to be able to adjust too.

Question 2

Is it possible for power-sharing to take place between users and workers?

The straightforward answer is that it is possible but difficult. One relatively simple mechanism for getting that process going is to share biographies. A worker and user meeting for the first time can get off to a good start by telling each other about themselves – the user's story and the worker's story. At a later stage they may both tell the biography

45

of the project to somebody else – the project's story. Knowing each other's background on equal terms can mark the beginning of a relationship that offers support to the individual and strength to the evolving community service.

WHAT'S IN A NAME?

As indicated at the start of this chapter how you are described as the consumer of a service can be very important. It is equally important that consideration is given to the name of a particular project or group. Such terms or names are closely associated with individual and group identity, a crucial factor in determining both internal feelings and external perceptions.

Language itself is a powerful force and once words have been used as descriptive terms changing them can be very difficult. It is not just the formal language or descriptions that are powerful, but the casual and informal ones too. For example in the mental health field, terms like 'schizo' or 'nutter' are probably more pervasive and damaging than patient or client. However, an exploration of this issue comes up with some surprising findings. Words and titles which professional people find uncomfortable turn out to be acceptable to consumer groups, and other words which on the face of it seem bland and innocent turn out to have negative images to those people being described.

There are also variations from region to region and country to country. I once visited a Drug and Alcohol project in Amsterdam at a time when the word client was being criticised in Britain and de-clienting social work was in vogue. The project director told me with great excitement that in Holland they were at last getting rid of the dreadful word patient, and were using the more positive word client!

Taking time to come to decisions about descriptive terms, job titles and the names of community projects is usually time well spent. The process of agreeing such terms and the listening involved may be more important than the actual decision taken. Community projects seem to benefit from having a name rather than being Blandford Mental Health Centre or Exshire Senior Citizens Mobile Lunch Club. It will certainly make interesting research for future historians to discover how a particular name was decided. Who would guess, for example, that a day centre called The Mill was originally run in church premises where the minister was called Alan Grist?

Some negative examples

Scratching off some wrapping paper from a home-made money box in an elderly person's loft, I was intrigued to find that it had originally been a collecting box for the Waifs and Strays Society. Further enquiry revealed that this eventually became the Church of England Children's Society, later to be shortened to the Childrens Society. This seems a good example of how important it is for voluntary organisations to move with the times and not leave themselves stuck with an out-of-date name or project title.

A more recent example of an inappropriate title is SANE (Schizophrenia a National Emergency). Despite the cleverness of the acronym and its apparent acceptability to professionals and other well-meaning people, patients and other users of mental health services were deeply hurt and angered by a title that assumed people to be insane.

The final negative example is of a different kind. It is the title of a workshop run at a conference where half the delegates were users. The workshop title was 'Care Coordination and Case Management with the Continued Care Client'. This had clearly been constructed to convey the content of the workshop accurately, but the impact on the users who attended was very negative. The kindest description I heard was that it was 'gobbledegook'.

Some positive examples

When you start looking for positive examples of titles and terminology there are also surprises in store. People might think that the *Madness Network News* was as old and outmoded as the Waifs and Strays Society, but it was 'a newsletter in newspaper format covering the ex-patients movement in North America and around the world' which ran from 1972 to 1986 (Chamberlin, 1987). More recently a group of mental health 'survivors' in Oxford (UK) have called their magazine *Libellus Dementum* (The Magazine of the Mad). In both instances it was clearly the members' choice to identify themselves in this way.

Other organisations can be quoted which demonstrate how direct you can be if you are deciding a name for yourself. Hearing Voices (mental health), Re-Think for Disabled People (physical disability), and People First (learning disability) are all examples of organisations where the people using a service have decided what to call themselves. This is the most important point in the whole debate, whether the question is about what you should be called personally, or what an organisation should be called. The choice should be yours.

CONCLUSIONS

Drawing conclusions from thinking and writing about this topic is not a tidy task, but there are five broad themes which can be identified:

- increased user empowerment has political implications;
- mutual empowerment and empowerment exchange are important concepts;
- people need training to improve their empowerment skills;
- the process of empowerment may be as important as the outcome;
- voluntary organisations should be taking the lead.

Political implications

A common feature of consumer run voluntary organisations is lack of money. This does not necessarily prevent a group from getting started, but it frequently holds back developments and keeps the group in a relatively powerless position. One commentator fears that the new style of funding could put the consumer involvement movement into reverse. 'The introduction of a market style of operation may even reverse the efforts that have been made in this sector towards involving more members of the consumer community in the running of local projects and services' (Taylor, 1992). She suggests that while in principle there is no reason why contract funding and market theory should prevent groups of consumers acting together, 'right of centre thinking is suspicious of the allocation of government or charitable money for such purposes'.

The question then arises as to who should be sustaining and developing the user movement within the voluntary sector. Should large voluntary organisations or umbrella bodies take a leading role?

Should 'pluralist' organisations which have both consumers and non-consumers as members be at the forefront? It seems clear that professionals should not lead the user movement, but should use their influence and resources to assist consumer groups to find their own direction.

Such a view is taken by Liz Sayce who sees user empowerment as 'the good news' in the development of community care. She thinks that the movement needs national co-ordinating bodies of users supported by established voluntary organisations which have opened themselves up to user participation and shared management (Sayce, 1991).

There is a real political dilemma here. Truly separatist groups will struggle for funds and recognition and are likely to become marginalised in a society rooted in class division, establishment power, professional dominance and respect for hierarchy. The tactic therefore has to be to operate on several fronts at the same time. Some of these fronts might be small local groups with a clear identity supported by pluralist organisations from the same field, training in political skills for key individuals, national movements to stimulate the whole debate and provide support and encouragement, user participation in the planning of the next generation of community services, and widening the debate within political parties, professional bodies and higher education.

Mutual empowerment and empowerment exchange

Historically power was felt to come from the barrel of a gun, and more recently in the film script language of *Godfather Three* it was decreed that 'real power cannot be given, it has to be taken'. The options outlined in this chapter are not so brutal but can be equally dramatic. Although the idea of empowerment exchange is a difficult one it is possible to visualise between individuals with different roles as well as within groups of people with a common goal. Adult education offers a good example. The educator may exchange some of her authority, influence and knowledge for a student's ideas, commitment and responsibility. The outcome may be a modified curriculum, an improvement in resources, or simply an opportunity for mutual learning and increased self-confidence.

One of the dilemmas, of course, is that the empowering person (e.g. teacher, social worker, doctor, project leader) may be a relatively powerless person outside a particular role or a particular relationship. This is where the notion of mutual empowerment is relevant. The parties concerned have to work out what level of empowerment is possible, who is the one more likely to exercise influence, and what other supporting bodies can be drawn into the process.

This is clearly a risky business. There are no guarantees that it will work or even that people will feel better for trying. Kate Harvey describes this dilemma in direct language;

> Empowerment necessitates risks. Risks for the organisation, risks for the users, risks for the workers. Risks like people leaving the building unlocked, setting off alarms, pinching tea money, or not returning borrowed items. But without risk there can be no responsibility.

> (Harvey, 1987)

Training to improve empowerment skills

Empowerment involves responsibility, and responsibility for even straightforward tasks is likely to require some degree of training. Deciding on your personal carers and interviewing them for appointment requires thought, experience and skill. Any organisation in the business of encouraging user involvement in this way needs to include training in its strategy. The training course devised with a group for physically disabled people in Croydon covered 'the basics of designing a job description, a person specification, and job advertisement. Trainees learn to plan, conduct and evaluate a selection interview, and they learn about equal opportunities, induction and health and safety' (Ogden, 1991).

Other skills which may need developing through training are: preparing for a meeting, speaking in a committee, chairing meetings, public speaking, listening to others, talking to professionals, writing articles, press releases and reports, using the telephone, and coping with aggression. Clearly this is not a definitive list, but it indicates the range of topics which need to be considered.

The process is as important as the outcome

Just as the travel plans and the journey may be the key to a good holiday, so the route from oppression to empowerment is as important as arriving. Stuart Rees has identified a number of stops along the way, the most important of which are:

- Learning how to express yourself and evaluate the self-image you uncover.

- Discovering how to make choices when the opportunity arises.

- Experiencing solidarity as a means of developing group power and reinforcing personal achievement.

- Knowing were to find information.

- Acquiring and using language.

- Evaluating how far alienation and isolation have been replaced by involvement and participation.

(Rees, 1991)

The strength which such a journey can give should not be underestimated.

The role of voluntary organisations

Although moves to involve consumers are being made in some statutory bodies, the majority of examples of effective user participation occur in voluntary organisations. This should be proudly proclaimed, both in the day-to-day negotiations for funds, premises and staff, and in the more public sphere of media contact, political liaison and community education. It is important that this leading role is maintained both because of its intrinsic worth and because there is much more still to be done.

REFERENCES

Ahmad B (1990) *Black Perspectives in Social Work*, Venture Press, Chapter 2

Barker I and Peck E (1987) 'Thinking it Through' *Power in Strange Places*, Good Practices in Mental Health

Bowden D (1988) *User Involvement in Mental Health Services: the Service Provider's Perspective*, Report of Common Concerns Conference, MIND

Brandon D (1991) *Direct Power: a Handbook on Service Brokerage,* TAO Publications

Chamberlin J (1987) 'The Case for Separatism – in Power in Strange Places' in I Barker & E Peck (eds) *Good Practices in Mental Health*

—— (1988) *On Our Own,* MIND Publications

Croft S and Beresford P (1990) *From Paternalism to Participation: Involving People in Social Services,* Open Services Project

Freire P (1972) *Pedagogy of the Oppressed,* Penguin

Fromm E (1960) *Fear of Freedom,* Routledge and Kegan Paul

George M (1991) 'Do It Yourself', *Community Care,* 9 May

Harvey K (1987) 'Steps Towards Autonomy' in I Barker and E Peck (eds) *Power in Strange Places,* Good Practices in Mental Health

Heginbotham (1990) *Return to Community,* Bedford Square Press

Lawson M (1988) *Individual Need – Collective Action, in Common Concerns,* Report on International Conference on User Involvement in Mental Health Services

Ogden J (1991) 'Reversal of Fortune', *Social Work Today,* 25 April

Rees S (1991) *Achieving Power: Practice and Policy in Social Welfare,* Allen & Unwin

Robson G (1987) 'Nagging – Models of Advocacy' in I Barker and E Peck (eds) *Power in Strange Places,* Good Practices in Mental Health

Sayce L (1991) *Waiting for Community Care,* MIND Publications

Taylor M (1992) 'The Changing Role of the Nonprofit Sector in Britain: Moving Toward the Market' in B Gidron *et al* (eds) *Government and the Third Sector,* Jossey-Bass

4
Voluntary organisations and Black communities

There are a number of important reasons for including this chapter, not least the fact that the needs and aspirations of Black self-help groups and voluntary organisations have been neglected in the past. Taking the issue seriously is a challenge to the voluntary sector as a whole, particularly to those groups and organisations that have evolved with white membership, white assumptions and the needs of white consumers as the focus of concern.

Two particularly positive reasons are suggested for putting the topic as a major theme. First, the development of Black voluntary organisations gives the voluntary sector as a whole something to celebrate. Second, it can be argued that Black voluntary organisations are a resource for change and social progress.

Steve Phaure suggests that much of the work undertaken by Black groups is 'innovative and highly original, it also represents an alternative to standard forms of provision, variously described as "holistic", "integrated" or "universal" ' (Phaure, 1991, p8). He argues that this distinctiveness has not been the cause of celebration which it should have been, either within or outside the voluntary sector.

That Black voluntary organisations are a resource for change is more difficult to argue. They are certainly in the forefront of local challenges and community issues and see themselves as more political and anti-racist than their white counterparts. Bandana Ahmad puts this role in historical perspective by quoting the community's response to an epidemic of yellow fever in Philadelphia in 1793. 'The Black community was so much better organised and equipped than the white community for caregiving that the white community turned to the Black community for salvation' (Ahmad B, 1990, p78).

She goes on to argue that Black workers and Black community groups have knowledge, experience and expertise so far untapped by the majority of white-dominated statutory agencies. Their potential as an instrument of social change and social justice is clear but whether this potential can become a significant political force is still to be determined.

A DEFINITION OF BLACK COMMUNITIES

Before proceeding any further a definition is called for. This is particularly important as a white writer exploring a Black theme. I intend to echo Steve Phaure in suggesting that 'Black' is used in both a generic and political sense to include African, Caribbean and Asian people and other people who would identify themselves as Black. I see it as a positive descriptive term. Using the term 'Black Communities' does not imply that the Black community is a homogeneous group, or that Black culture is unitary or monolithic. However, it is likely that Black groups and organisations will share certain experiences, such as racism and discrimination, which give them a special identity and communal bonding.

SIGNIFICANT FEATURES OF BLACK VOLUNTARY ORGANISATIONS

There are two connected features which stand out in the development of Black community groups and voluntary organisations. First groups tend to identify themselves with their ethnicity rather than a particular social problem, and second, the services provided are more wide-ranging and less confined to specific needs such as housing, disability or old age.

Both Ahmad and Phaure found Black voluntary organisations covering a wider range of community services than their white equivalents. The term 'holistic' is used to convey a bringing together of services rather than a separation into specialist fields of community care. 'Holistic services approach issues like mental health, racism and housing as being inter-related, requiring a multi-faceted rather than a compartmentalised response' (Phaure, 1991, p36).

This tendency is found not only in community groups whose origins lie in community solidarity, but also in groups set up for a specific purpose. The United Anglo-Caribbean Society in Ealing, for example, was originally set up by parents who were dissatisfied with their children's education and determined to develop a supplementary schooling system. Within two years, in the holistic tradition, new services were emerging in the form of youth clubs, advice services and a luncheon club, as well as a Saturday school run by volunteer teachers (Phaure, 1991).

One major problem of this otherwise beneficial tradition is that financial support tends to be directed towards groups meeting identifiable social problems rather than generic or holistic organisations. Thus in Ealing the emphasis has latterly been focused on providing services for the elderly as this was more likely to be supported financially by the local council. As will be seen with other examples, even being more focused does not readily bring in the required funding.

ALTERNATIVE MODELS OF BLACK VOLUNTARY ORGANISATIONS

It is useful to examine the different models of voluntary organisations with a significant Black component and see what they have to offer. The three models most regularly described are:

(a)   Black self-help groups;

(b)   Black community groups with some paid workers;

(c)   Mixed community groups providing some specific services for Black people but established for the local white population.

Black self-help groups

Such groups often arise from a feeling of neglect and need the initiative of one or two key people with confidence, influence and a sense of community responsibility. They are most often found in such ventures as lunch clubs for older people or groups with a cultural emphasis. They are often the starting point for projects which get bigger and begin to provide a wider range of services. An example of such a project is the West Indian Women's Association in Brent. This was started by a small group of women who organised discussion groups and events celebrating African Caribbean culture and cuisine. The Association went on to include a far wider range of activities such as youth work, work with the elderly, work with the unemployed and spiritual counselling (Phaure, 1991).

Black community groups

These groups are the best examples of the holistic or integrated organisations referred to earlier. Some are relatively small such as the Black Carers Support Group in Lozells, Birmingham, but others have grown to encompass a large number of families and services. An example of the latter is Southall Contact a Family which provides short-term respite care for nearly 200 Asian families who have children with special needs. In the holistic tradition the organisation not only provides a wide range of playschemes, children's clubs, parents' workshops and family outings, but now goes beyond its original brief to arrange cultural events and a walk-in service offering advice on benefits, education and domestic violence (Phaure, 1991).

Although much smaller the Black Carers Support Group also does more than its original role of providing social support to a vulnerable group of carers. Workers help members to liaise with the statutory services, provide advocacy and learn how to speak at public meetings and conferences (Fielding, 1990).

Another example of a small Black community group is the Elim House Day Centre in Peckham, south-east London. This provides a day care service on five days per week for up to thirty people per day with an emphasis on Caribbean food, music, dancing and other activities. White people are not prevented from using the centre and one of the keenest attenders went originally with a Black friend. A key motivating factor for many of those attending was the avoidance of racism, something all had experienced in white or mixed race facilities (Heptinstall, 1989).

Mixed community groups

Modifying a white facility to provide an adequate service for people from Black communities is notoriously difficult. It is even difficult to communicate the role and purpose of a community project if such a scheme seems alien to a particular group of people. An example from my own experience which seems embarrassing in retrospect was to write to various Asian community leaders enclosing leaflets about a mental-health day centre written in three Asian languages. Receiving such information out of the blue brought mixed reactions. One was full of praise for including them in the circulation while another who visited on the same day was highly indignant at the implication that any members of his temple might be mad.

The most successful mixed schemes seem to be those where a special service has been added to whatever was there before and it is essential to involve and probably employ someone from the Black community as a development worker. The National Schizophrenia Fellowship's 'Man Sangathan Project' in Ealing is a good example of such a specialist service set up by an erstwhile white organisation. It was set up 'to provide specific services to people of Asian descent'. The project aims to provide an interpreting and advocacy service for people with mental illness and their carers by recruiting and training volunteers. It also runs an advisory service in Punjabi, Hindi and Urdu, using a telephone help-line. This service covers housing, legal issues, social services, and money problems. The project co-ordinator comes from the Asian community but the management group includes white professionals as well as a representative of the local Racial Equality Council (Phaure, 1991).

Particular problems for Black voluntary organisations

Highlighting particular problems for Black voluntary organisations is not necessarily a negative exercise – a bit depressing, perhaps, but designed to bring out for both current and potential groups the realities of community care for Black communities.

The most obvious of all the problems is lack of money. This is an issue for all voluntary organisations but seems particularly problematic for Black communities. One reason for this seems to be the holistic nature of many projects and the wish to be flexible and responsive to new needs as they arise. Funding bodies, particularly in an era of the purchaser-provider divide, tend to look for services providing a specific service or meeting the needs of a particular group of clients. Some organisations therefore find that only a small part of their overall programme attracts funds or they feel forced into changing the focus of their work in order to meet the terms of a contract.

Traditional funding mechanisms can prevent groups from developing on their own terms and in the interests of their membership. The NCVO *Newsletter* in July 1991 identified one group where statutory funding was the beginning of the end. Their aims and flexibility were said to be compromised and they felt they could not determine their own fate or the areas of work which they thought were important.

Bandana Ahmad, from the perspective of the Race Equality Unit at the National Institute for Social Work, suggests that 'Black organisations have severely restricted resources and insecurity compared to most mainstream voluntary organisations' (Ahmad, 1988).

Phaure's study also came to the conclusion that Black organisations had more difficulty getting funds than white organisations. He also felt that white organisations could impede the development of appropriate Black groups by trying to provide an integrated service themselves. Certainly fitting the aspirations of Black communities into the current model of community care and the matching funding systems is fraught with difficulties.

Another problem that seems to be endemic is racism, both individual and institutional. Even the most charming and endearing person in an all-white context can come over as racist when part of multi-racial gathering. Similarly, organisations which have happily gone along believing themselves to be forward thinking, enlightened and flexible discover that they are part of a racist state with no easy way out of their historically induced culture. Some of the Black projects discussed earlier in the chapter put this forward as the primary reason for setting up a separate scheme or organisation.

The media are another problem for Black communities and not only the tabloid press. It was particularly unfortunate when the regular Channel 4 programme *The Black Bag* looked at the financing of Black voluntary organisations in London. In 'The Grants Game' of November 1991 they chose to concentrate on a few negative examples where 'millions of pounds are being squandered on voluntary groups that are out of control'. The opportunity to investigate the long tradition of racism in the boroughs concerned was not taken nor was there the broader picture of soundly based Black voluntary groups struggling to obtain finance.

The final problem to note is the difficulty, both linguistically and culturally, of interpreting the needs of Black communities. Good communication is needed both within Black communities and between

Black communities and community care services. A major problem within Black communities may be the difficulty of finding adequate teaching facilities for traditional languages and for religious education. According to a Report on Languages published in 1982 by the Commission for Racial Equality, Preston's two mosques were struggling to teach Urdu and Arabic to a student population of 920 with 34 teachers, of whom only 2 were paid.

This dependence on voluntary teachers and voluntary organisations to take responsibility for basic second-language skills is a striking feature of many Black communities. Not only are they dependent on voluntary workers, but even the minimal funds needed to rent premises and provide books and equipment may be difficult to raise.

Interpreting needs to white workers and explaining to Black families what services are available is the other major linguistic problem. In examining how to improve mental health services for Black communities, Yvonne Christie and Roger Blunden say that 'good interpreting is required for people whose first language is not English. Clear understanding of what people are trying to communicate is particularly important in mental health, since it forms the basis of much diagnosis and therapy' (Christie and Blunden, 1991).

An attempt has been made in Liverpool to bridge the communication gap between Black communities and health workers. It is significant that the scheme which has been set up relies on volunteers who are all professional workers in their paid role. Between them the 47 volunteers can interpret in 14 different languages, the major problem being how to arrange a convenient time when all three parties can meet (Fewster, 1989).

ARE THERE ANY ENCOURAGING SIGNS FOR BLACK COMMUNITIES?

Despite the problems outlined above there are some positive developments to encourage both Black voluntary organisations and others in the voluntary sector who want to see progress made. The first of these to be noted is the very general point that an increasing feature of daily life in Britain is to have clothes, food, music, art, places of worship, shops and restaurants which reflect a variety of cultures and ethnic backgrounds. This variety pervades the lives of young and old, making a rich mix and a wonderful opportunity to enjoy different customs and practices. I am sure the old adage applies that 'you can take a horse to water but you can't make it drink', but it is hard for even the most committed fish and chip freak to resist the delights of food from China, India, the Caribbean and Mexico.

A more down-to-earth but still important issue is that certain legislation is beginning to reflect the needs of citizens from Black communities. An example of this is The Children Act 1989. Within the central theme of the act that the welfare of the child is paramount, social workers have legal obligations to promote the welfare of Black children in ways that meet his or her ethnic needs. As Bandana Ahmad points out:

> The Children Act 1989 is the first legislation regarding children that includes not just religion, but three other important factors as well – a child's racial origin, ethnicity and linguistic background. This has major implications for social workers and authorities, as it will be unlawful to ignore the race, culture, language and religion of children who are looked after by statutory and voluntary institutions.

> (Ahmad B, 1990, p89)

The impact on legislation is a slow one, and it is disappointing to note that few of the recommendations submitted by the Race Equality Unit of the National Institute for Social Work found their way into the National Health Service and Community Care Act 1990.

There are other ways of bringing about change in social policy other than through legislation and one example of this is the change taking place in social work education. The requirements for the Diploma in Social Work (CCETSW Paper 30) identify issues of race not only in the knowledge base, but in the competencies which each student is required to demonstrate in their practice.

What is even more encouraging is that the guidelines on how this should be done are no longer based on polarised positions but show that it is possible to examine race both as a political issue demanding anti-racist strategies and as a professional practice issue requiring an understanding of the needs of different cultural groups in a multi-cultural society (Naik, 1991).

These background issues may aid some of the more specific changes which are taking place in the voluntary sector. The evidence seems to be that the newer Black projects and agencies seem to be more accessible to Black communities than either statutory bodies or old-style voluntary organisations. A recent study by Jayanthi Beliappa on how people from the Asian community in the London Borough of Haringey react to mental illness and related social problems threw up some interesting findings. Only 13 per cent of the sample saw their family as a durable support structure in tackling their difficulties and a tiny proportion, 3 per cent, saw statutory services as a means of help. On the other hand 32 per cent said they would seek help from the voluntary sector (Beliappa, 1991). Although these figures demonstrate that neither formal nor informal social systems are seen to be useful for a majority of the sample interviewed, at least the voluntary sector is seen as accessible by a significant minority.

A further encouraging sign is that some statutory agencies are beginning to take Black voluntary organisations more seriously. The official line from the National Institute for Social Work to Social Services Departments is that the relationship between them and Black community groups should be one of equal partnership. They are encouraged to use this partnership to help with administration, interpreting services, information and advice, research and training (Ahmad A, 1990).

There is, of course, a long way to go before guidance and exhortation become common practice. However, Black voluntary organisations are clearly on the social policy agenda. It remains to be seen whether they reach the top of the agenda or stay as 'Any other business'.

The final point of optimism to mention relates to the existence of The Organisation Development Unit or ODU. This is a national Black voluntary sector development agency rooted in the experience and aspirations of the Black voluntary sector. Originally set up as part of the National Council for Voluntary Organisations it became independent of NCVO in 1991. Its aims are to help Black voluntary groups increase their effectiveness and to influence institutional policies which affect the Black voluntary sector. ODU provides training, information and support with funding applications and it clearly sees its brief as including political influence. With over 2000

Black groups on its mailing list it has the potential to be a significant force in the development of the Black voluntary sector.

REFERENCES

Ahmad A (1990) *Practice with Care*, Race Equality Unit, NISW

Ahmad B (1988) 'When Sharing Assumptions Can Pave the Way to Partnership', *Social Work Today*, Vol. 20, No. 15

—— (1990) Black Perspectives in Social Work, Venture Press

Beliappa J (1991) *Illness or Distress? Alternative Models of Mental Health*, Confederation of Indian Organisations (UK)

Christie Y and Blunden R (1991) *Is Race on Your Agenda?* King's Fund Centre

Fewster C (1989) 'Trying to Speak in Tongues', *The Health Service Journal* 27 July

Fielding N (1990) 'A Group with a Difference', *Community Care* 11 January

Heptinstall D (1989) 'Black and White Choice for Elderly Consumers', *Social Work Today*, 24 August

Naik D (1991) 'Towards an Antiracist Curriculum in Social Work Training' in *One Small Step Towards Racial Justice* CCETSW

Phaure S (1991) *Who Really Cares? Models of Voluntary Sector Community Care and Black Communities*, London Voluntary Service Council

5
Relationships with the statutory sector

The hand that gives is always above the hand that receives.

(Turkish Proverb)

The original idea was to call this chapter 'The Partnership between the Voluntary and Statutory Sectors'. However, the term partnership is so full of assumptions and expectations that in the end a more neutral word had to be found. Not that the word relationship is free from such assumptions and expectations, it just seems more appropriate.

This chapter starts with an exploration of the idea of partnership and the variety of ways in which the concept can be interpreted. It then examines the political relationships which are involved, including the imbalance of power and the growing influence of the business community. This is followed by sections on financial issues and on the particular relationship between local government and local voluntary organisations. The joint planning system is discussed as an example of where the two sectors meet for so-called planning purposes, and this is followed by a comment on the growing significance of other organisations, particularly those in the private and not-for-profit sectors. The chapter ends by posing questions about whether the voluntary and statutory sectors can be partners in development, not only at a local level but in a national and international context.

THE PARTNERSHIP PRINCPLE

Writing in 1985 Maria Brenton was sceptical about the idea of partnership and the significance of voluntary organisations in the field of community care.

> The understanding of 'partnership' as a collaborative
> relationship between local authorities and local voluntary

organisations through which each carries a joint responsibility for planning, policy-making and implementation as part of a whole, and where voluntary agencies enjoy parity of status and influence, is one that exists more in theory than in reality.

(Brenton, 1985, p128)

By 1989 the White Paper *Caring for People* envisaged a new climate of partnership between local authorities and the voluntary sector and this principle was enshrined in the following National Health Service and Community Care Act (1990).

What does this principle of partnership mean in practice? According to Ralph Kramer it means a series of transactions of four different types. These are:

a) fiscal (grants, fees, indirect, in-kind); b) regulatory (standard setting and licensing); c) service delivery (exchange of information, referrals, consultations, coordination and planning, contracts and joint operations); d) political (advocacy or campaigning).

(Kramer, 1990, p44)

This breakdown is useful both because it distinguishes the reasons for such partnerships and because it indicates likely conflict of interest between the different transactions. How much voluntary organisations hold back in their political transactions because of inhibitions caused by other transactions is largely unknown, but it is clearly significant in the development of a partnership or working relationship.

Exploring this idea further, Kramer suggests a continuum in these working relationships ranging from: 'joint operations, joint planning and coordination, purchase of service, cooperative arrangements, accommodation, coexistence, to competition and conflict' (ibid.). Such a list can be criticised for being just a string of words, but it begins to separate out the different components of the partnership. For individual voluntary organisations as well as their statutory partners this unravelling of the knotted ball of wool which partnerships have become is a preliminary to getting the relationship on to a stronger footing.

Through the National Council for Voluntary Organisations the voluntary sector has made several attempts to clarify its own position in relation to community care and the partnership with the statutory sector. Various reports and articles come over as purposeful, earnest and succinct but tend to simplify some of the operational difficulties which organisations experience at both national and local level.

What has to be recognised is that the partnership is not one of equals, nor even of similar organisations. It is something akin to a school of whales trying to relate to a collection of octopuses – a group of heavy mammals swimming in uncharted waters followed by other creatures with one cooperative tentacle, one critical tentacle and six unsure whether to cling on or swim away.

To put the dilemma in a more orthodox way, are voluntary organisations partners at all or are they merely agents? By their very nature voluntary organisations are without both statutory authority and statutory obligation yet they want to be involved in statutory planning and the provision of statutory services. Is this one of the paradoxes of a liberal, democratic society with an implicit commitment to the care of its citizens? Or is it the obscuring tactic of an élitist, dictatorial establishment wanting to keep power in its own hands and give little away to collective community care?

POLITICAL RELATIONSHIPS

The political and power relationships among and between statutory authorities and voluntary organisations are crucial factors in discovering the true nature of the partnership. On the surface there seems to be a consensus between the three main political parties in Great Britain that supporting the voluntary sector is a good idea. As though to emphasise the partnership principle the Labour Party's document prior to the 1992 general election was called *Building Bridges*. The Conservative government's response to the efficiency scrutiny of government funding of the voluntary sector is entitled *Profiting from Partnership*, and the equivalent Liberal Democrat document is headed *Agenda for Caring*.

On the margins there is a difference between the government party and the opposition so far as the voluntary sector's role as critic and pressure group is concerned. The Labour Party document describes campaigning on and behalf of beneficiaries and members as 'essential to a healthy democracy, providing a voice for those who otherwise remain unheard'. This echoes the views of the National Council for Voluntary Organisations who in their *Newsletter* for January 1992 welcomed Labour's plans.

The public commitment of a major political party to partnership with the voluntary sector at all the levels described by Kramer above is important in the long term, even if a cynic would say that making promises is always easier when you are in opposition. The Conservative party is less happy with the policy-making and campaigning aspects of the partnership, although the then party chairman was in favour in 1991 of 'using them as a sounding board and milking them of ideas' (Deakin, 1991). Apart from the dissonance of a mixed metaphor there is also within that comment the assumption of government as decision-takers or farm managers and voluntary organisations as service providers or a herd of compliant cattle.

The government's position and that which any party would feel obliged to take once in government is that 'the government alone cannot resolve all the problems of society nor can it enhance the quality of life to its fullest for everyone' (HMSO, February 1992, p36). This stems from a policy that 'seeks a free, vigorous and creative partnership with the voluntary sector, in which both parties can make their distinctive and valuable contributions' (ibid., p7).

The question that has to be asked following such a statement, is how free, vigorous and creative is it possible to be? One commentator is clear that the voluntary sector is 'in danger of being taken over or colonised by the new welfare ideology brought about by the Conservative governments of the 1980s, not in any absolute sense of ownership but in the ownership of ideas and philosophy' (Hall, 1989).

The challenge to voluntary organisations stemming from this point of view is how to avoid becoming part of the establishment. The requirements to meet contract criteria, the need to manage the organisation efficiently, and the pressure to align with the political values of the moment all point to some organisations being favoured and others being out in the cold.

It also points to a lack of influence on legislation and political decision-taking. The Local Government Finance Bill which was being debated in the run up to the general election of 1992 was the kind of legislation which the voluntary sector would have to influence if it was to think of itself as being in active partnership with government. In practice, despite efficient priming of spokespersons in the House of Lords, no changes were forthcoming on vital issues such as rate relief for charities, rate capping of money committed to voluntary organisations, local authority planning in respect of voluntary sector funding, and securing budget dates for decisions about local government grants and fees.

A small scale-study by Clark showed a similar lack of influence on policy decisions in the field of employment. (Clark, 1991) Eight projects working in partnership with the Manpower Services Commission in Scotland were surveyed and the author concludes that the relationship between the MSC and the eight voluntary organisations 'was seldom harmonious and bore all the stigma of unequal compromise between fundamentally different aspirations'. He also notes that there is little evidence of state provision being improved because of either the example or representations made by these voluntary organisations (Clark, 1991).

An important additional political influence which needs to be considered is the business community. The Conservative administration in Great Britain is clear that the business community has an important part to play in the development of voluntary organisations. In their 1992 document on the role of the voluntary sector it is explicitly stated that: 'The concept of the active citizen extends from the individual to the corporate sector, embracing the idea of the corporate sector's exercising wider responsibilities in the community' (HMSO, 1992, p35).

Community investment is seen not just as philanthropic, an optional extra, but as a core part of business for sound commercial reasons. The HMSO document lists a large number of social goals which would be mutually beneficial for industry, the voluntary sector and the community as a whole, but one wonders how many commercial bodies are open to these arguments. John Patten, when minister at the Home Office responsible for the Voluntary Services Unit, argued that there should be an exchange of business skills between the business and voluntary sectors.

Patten's view, like that of many commentators, is that the main expertise lies with the business sector so that 'voluntary groups inevitably benefit from the process, but so too do businesses, because individual executives are given a rare opportunity to develop their career potential in a new and testing work environment' (Patten, 1991, p10). A casual observation of this process leads to the conclusion that those people given this 'opportunity' tend to be staff who are on their way out of the organisation or are 'misfits' rather than people who are central to the business mission or enterprise culture.

A more positive view of the potential of cooperation comes in the NCVO document *What Local Groups Need* published in 1990. In describing the relationship between local voluntary groups and the corporate sector as 'symbiotic', the report suggests that: 'Local voluntary groups can help a business become more efficient and effective and that companies in turn can help local groups become more efficient and effective by offering company expertise, grants, employee involvement, company facilities, and help in kind.'

The expertise offered by the voluntary sector to the business sector includes: helping company staff to set up counselling, pre-retirement courses, victim support schemes etc., offering staff opportunities to do voluntary work, developing joint child-care programmes, recruitment packages, training schemes, and recreational activities, offering advice and information about local facilities for the benefit of staff, and offering local sponsorship deals which give companies marketing opportunities. As if to demonstrate this last point the cover states discreetly that the report is sponsored by NatWest, The Action Bank.

The final partnership to consider in this section is perhaps the most significant – the relationship between central government and local government. As discussed in Chapter 2 and later in this chapter, local voluntary organisations have traditionally been dependent on local government but until relatively recently local government has had some discretion in deciding local political priorities. During the 1980s and early 1990s this local autonomy had gradually been whittled away, first by the abolition of the Greater London Council and the Metropolitan Counties in 1985, and more recently by the stranglehold on local authority spending

FINANCIAL RELATIONSHIPS

Financial relationships between the voluntary and statutory sectors are clearly dependent on the political relationships which underpin them. Two themes stand out in examining such relationships. First the unwillingness of government to put its money where its mouth is, and second, the relative weakness of local government as a financial partner.

When published in April 1990, the Efficiency Scrutiny of Government Funding of the Voluntary Sector was widely welcomed by voluntary organisations. It was seen as a vindication of criticisms that grants administration had been unsatisfactory and made significant recommendations to enhance the status of voluntary sector funding as a key aspect of government policy. The partnership principle was underlined by the suggestion that 'funding programmes are more likely to achieve value for money where there is a shared commitment to objectives' (Hunter, 1990).

Hunter also makes the point that the report focuses on the need for government departments to take a more strategic view of the way funding programmes contribute to overall policy objectives. The voluntary sector should have its views taken into account as new policy initiatives are planned, and financial incentives should be used to encourage local and health authorities to make better use of the potential of voluntary organisations to deliver services.

The government document responding to the Efficiency Scrutiny can only be described as pathetic. A year after the Scrutiny was published the Voluntary Services Unit at the Home Office produced a six-page report deftly avoiding any political commitment and presented in such a low-key way that few people realised it had happened. It demonstrates clearly that financing the voluntary sector is a very low political priority. The concluding paragraph says that 'the general principles are accepted as applicable and departments will be moving in the direction recommended by the report' (Voluntary Services Unit, 1991). Clearly Sir Humphrey is alive and well!

The financial weakness of local government in Britain is the other main problem for voluntary organisations. This clearly applies particularly to local service-providing and co-ordinating groups which have traditionally struggled to obtain long-term financial commitments from local authorities. Kramer sees the problems as 'voluntary agencies confronted by a weakened enabler-partner' stifled by rate-capping and charge-capping. The net result is 'a dangerous threat to the survival of small, community based organisations' (Kramer, 1990, p52).

NCVO makes similar points in reviewing the impact of the Poll Tax on voluntary organisations. Even when there is a partnership of principle and policy in developing community care local authorities and local voluntary organisations are hamstrung.

The structure and funding of local government are key determinants of this partnership. A local government finance system which results in dramatic cuts in local expenditure, such as the poll tax system, clearly has a very damaging effect on investment in the infrastructure for local voluntary action – without which it is impossible to develop and sustain effective partnerships.

(NCVO, 1991, p6)

NCVO News throughout 1991 and 1992 showed that voluntary organisations lost almost £30 million in local authority funding, that local development agencies lost £3.2 million, that 32 local authorities had reduced budgets for social services in that year, and that the projected loss to voluntary organisations of local authority funding in 1992–3 was £42.4 million. These figures are devastating, both as an indictment of social policy and in the direct impact on a large number of local voluntary groups. They fly in the face of the exhortation in the White Paper *Caring for People* that Local Authorities should give them (voluntary organisations) a sounder financial base and allow them a greater degree of certainty in planning for the future. Simon Hebditch suggests that contradictory forces are at work in central government.

It appears that the two arms of government are resolutely marching in opposite directions. The Department of Health wishes to encourage increased voluntary sector involvement in the provision of services and indeed sees voluntary organisations as a partner alongside the public and private sectors in this field. On the other hand, the Department of the Environment is requiring local authorities to cut back on services in order to meet the parameters laid down in their standard spending assessments.

(Hebditch, 1992)

THE FUTURE OF LOCAL GOVERNMENT

Voluntary organisations, particularly local agencies and community groups, are so dependent of their relationship with local authorities that it is particularly important to try and understand the direction which local government is likely to take during the 1990s. In a particularly succinct examination of the changing relationship between local government and the voluntary sector, Gutch, Kunz and Spencer identify two possible directions for local government in Britain.

The first option is a reducing political force which is 'retracting in on itself, concentrating on improving the quality of the services it has left and limiting its concerns to its statutory responsibilities – what happens to the rest of the community is not its concern' (Gutch, *et al.*, 1990, p5).

The alternative view is described as 'community governance in the broadest sense', providing community leadership, co-ordination of services, democratic accountability, and a fair and efficient monitoring service. This requires the balancing a number of conflicting roles (e.g. direct service provider, regulator, contractor, community representative, and enabler) (ibid., p5)

The dilemma for the voluntary sector is that while the latter perspective is clearly preferable, the trend is distinctly towards the former. There is therefore not only uncertainty about what the future will bring, but a sense of foreboding that the direction being taken by local government will lead to a similar retraction in the voluntary sector itself.

When it works well the partnership between local government and the voluntary sector is mutually supportive, involves consultation about both the planning and delivery of services, and allows advocacy and campaigning to be an active ingredient of the voluntary sector's role. One litmus test of the value of the relationship is whether benefits are perceived as going both ways. Voluntary organisations have knowledge, skills and contacts which can be very useful to statutory bodies. Gutch and colleagues would like to see 'a more collaborative, consultative, style of working between local authorities and the voluntary sector especially in community care (Gutch *et al*, 1990, p5).

71

Kramer warns that in the era of a purchaser-supplier relationship between local government and voluntary organisations the latter need to beware of 'off-loading' and 'dumping' (Kramer, 1990, p52). This is clearly a danger where local authorities have insufficient resources or the lack of political will to fight the erosion of their authority. Some of the problems of differing values, language and the power imbalance can be tackled in a relatively straightforward way if both sides are willing to set out aims, objectives and principles openly, with a clear statement of what cannot be done as well as what can.

This was the experience on the Isle of Wight where the partnership between Community Service Volunteers and the Social Services Department demonstrated effective mobilisation of volunteers to help develop new models of community care (Harrison, 1991). While it is encouraging to read small-scale reports of progress being made the overall trend does not look so good. An examination of the Joint Planning System shows up the practical deficiencies in what, on paper, is a good idea.

THE JOINT PLANNING SYSTEM

Since 1974 when Joint Consultative Committees became a statutory mechanism for planning and financing joint community care initiatives, all parts of England and Wales have had joint planning schemes. Right from the start the only directly elected members of those JCCs have been people representing the voluntary sector. Health authority and local authority representatives have been appointed by their respective authorities and in the case of health authorities this has meant a complete lack of democratic accountability.

Voluntary sector representatives have tended to be the poor relations in this forum, partly because of their lack of experience in large formal bodies, and partly because they bring no cash to the table. The idea, of course, was that any money in the Joint Finance pot should acquire joint ownership including that of the voluntary sector. In practice health authorities have found it difficult not to view it as their money since the mechanism for distribution has been through the NHS funding system. Local authorities have also found this irksome from time to time.

A case study of one local authority's treatment of the voluntary sector involvement in joint planning makes interesting reading. In 1989 when the voluntary sector had got its act together by creating a Voluntary Sector Forum in Joint Planning it lobbied the statutory authorities to have a place on the Joint Consultative Planning Team, the body of senior officers where all major decisions were taken. After some reluctance this was agreed, but within six months the JCPT was abolished and replaced by a meeting of the three general managers of the Social Services Department, the District Health Authority and the new Family Health Services Authority.

After protests the voluntary sector was invited to send representatives to this meeting for particular agenda items and was encouraged to use the formal mechanism of the Joint Consultative Committee for discussion of major planning issues and the smaller joint planning groups for discussing local and client-focused topics. One would have therefore imagined that in the era of bringing to fruition the Community Care plans for the county, the JCC would have been a lively and vigorous forum for discussion. In fact members received letters for two consecutive quarterly meetings to say that: 'Following consultation with the Chairman the next meeting of the Joint Consultative Committee has been cancelled due to the lack of business to be discussed' (Oxfordshire JCC Minutes, 1989–1992).

While acknowledging that JCCs are often cumbersome and even boring, with serious questions about their ability to bring about change, the ease with which they can be pushed aside by thrusting managers should be a matter of concern not only to voluntary organisations but to elected members of local authorities. After two decades of a joint planning system it appears to be one of those good ideas which never really got off the ground. Despite reservations, some commentators think that the voluntary sector should stay actively involved in its operation.

> Taken together the JCPT and JCC provide rare opportunities for the voluntary sector to present its views to senior managers and members of statutory services. What is more, in the JCC we have our only legal right to membership of any group involved in the joint development of services. This is something we would not easily abandon.

> (McGee, 1991)

73

One dilemma in an era of presumed managerial efficiency is whether full participation by anybody, let alone the voluntary sector, is cost effective. Clearly there are contradictions between Department of Health policy guidelines which require that 'both health and local authorities shall involve voluntary and other organisations in the planning process' and a system which devolves planning and service provision to trusts, GP fundholders and private enterprise.

Another dilemma is the effect of the corporate management culture on the language, structure and operation of joint planning schemes. The case study mentioned earlier had moved by mid-1992 to a structure headed by a Joint Commissioning Group with 'membership limited to those who can bring money to the table'. This relegated the voluntary sector to representation on the 'Advisory Group', which includes users and carers, and the 'Managerial Group' for service providers.

The overall picture seems to be one of gradual dilution of voluntary sector involvement in the joint planning for community care. The last word in this section belongs to the Council for Voluntary Action from the local case study already discussed. In preparing a paper about the voluntary sector's role in planning, the director writes:

> Those involved formally in the process have felt bemused with
> the pace of change in relation to planning for care and
> sometimes demoralised by the seeming lack of commitment from
> statutory authorities to the joint planning process.

(OCVA, July 1992)

PARTNERS IN DEVELOPMENT

Development is one of those enticing words that implies social progress, moving forward and making changes for the better. When it works well that is what happens, and the voluntary sector can sometimes be very good at development.

The appointment of development workers is a good example of where the voluntary sector takes a good idea and then employs somebody to carry it out. So often in the statutory sector staff are asked to take on the implementation of good ideas on top of their other responsibilities. This means that the idea moves ahead very slowly and sometimes never becomes operational at all. Development workers are freed up to assess need, to create networks, to liaise with a wide range of professionals and consumers, and to start pilot projects. In the process of undertaking those tasks they can also be planning where to obtain funds for turning a pilot project into a continuing service.

As part of the networking process development workers spend a significant part of their time in contact with people at different levels of their organisations. This is another of their strengths in voluntary organisations. They are not confined to a particular level of interaction or hierarchy but can legitimately be negotiating with a senior manager one day and a consumer group the next.

The developmental role of voluntary organisations as a whole is also important, either when this is their specific role or when it is one of the tasks taken on in bringing the needs of the community to the notice of the statutory sector. There is an interesting irony in the situation where elected members of local authorities are dependent for knowledge of their communities on information given to them by community groups. That level of personal and political interaction is crucial if both the political system and the voluntary sector are going to have credibility at local level.

Finding appropriate mechanisms for developing this dialogue is one of the most important tasks for local government and the voluntary sector. As already demonstrated, the joint planning system has many flaws and ambiguities while less formal procedures may be effective in some places and non-existent in others.

One feature of official documents and legislation bringing the NHS and Community Care Act into operation is the way the voluntary sector has been merged with the private sector and not-for-profit organisations under the banner of the independent sector. There may be some benefit in setting up a local forum which includes all elements of this independent sector, but it is equally important for the voluntary sector to establish a clear and separate identity.

Gutch and colleagues suggest that voluntary organisations adopt a positive and proactive approach to the task of working more effectively with local government. They suggest doing this by taking advantage of consultation requirements of legislation and official guidelines, making clear statements about the strengths of the voluntary sector and living up to them, and by developing the 'infrastructure' needed in the form of local development and co-ordinating agencies (Gutch *et al*, 1990).

This would, of course, require a reciprocal response from local government including a willingness to fund some of that infrastructure. It would also require government at both national and local level to see 'citizenship strategies' applying to communities and community action not solely to the needs and minimal requirements of individuals (Gutch *et al*, 1990, p48).

The final word in this chapter is about the wider international implications of partnerships between voluntary organisations and government or supra-government agencies. At a strategic level formal mechanisms are already in place for communication between the voluntary sector in Europe and the various political and legal institutions effecting community care, with NCVO and The Charities Aid Foundation as the lead agencies.

At local level, however, contact between voluntary organisations in different countries is very small. Perhaps a system of twinning between relevant agencies in different countries is worth considering. International conferences are also a useful and instructive way of bringing people together, and the voluntary sector has already shown itself capable of setting up such initiatives in both the mental health field and with community care for elderly people.

REFERENCES

Brenton M (1985) *The Voluntary Sector in British Social Services*, Longman

Clark C L (1991) *Theory and Practice in Voluntary Social Action*, Avebury

Deakin N (1991) 'Government and the Voluntary Sector in the 1990s', *Policy Studies*, Autumn, Vol.12(3)

Gutch R, Kunz C & Spencer K (1990) *Partners or Agents?* National Council for Voluntary Organisations

Hall S (1989) *The Voluntary Sector Under Attack?* Islington Voluntary Action Council

Harrison H (1991) *An Experiment in Partnership*, CIS Commentary No. 38, Polytechnic of East London

Hebditch S (1992) 'Community Care in Crisis', *NCVO News*, March

HMSO (1992) *The Individual and The Community*, Home Office and Central Office of Information, February

Hunter J (1990) *The Efficiency Scrutiny and the Voluntary Sector*, ARVAC Bulletin, Summer

Kramer R (1990) *Change and Continuity in British Voluntary Organisations*, VOLUNTAS, November, Manchester University Press

McGee P (1991) 'Joint Planning at County Level', Community Care Newsletter, NCVO July

NCVO (1991) *Investing in Partnership*, National Council for Voluntary Organisations, February

Oxfordshire Council for Voluntary Action (1992) *Commissions, Purchasing, Providing – Planning for the Future*, OCVA

Patten J (1991) 'Government, Business and the Voluntary Sector: a Developing Partnership', *Policy Studies*, Autumn, Vol.12(3)

Voluntary Services Unit (1991) *Profiting from Partnership – the Implementation Process*, Home Office

6
The politics of voluntary organisations

PART I: OWNING OUR HISTORY

History and politics are inextricably mixed, and this final chapter attempts to show the importance of voluntary organisations owning their own history as well as finding an effective political role in the current era of social welfare. In examining this history four themes will be explored:

1 Voluntary organisations as a support to the political and moral establishment and a potential oppressor of the poor;

2 Their role as innovator, change agent and political irritant;

3 Coping with being both an insider and an outsider;

4 The lack of political support or interest except at times of national emergency.

Voluntary organisations as part of the establishment

Like many people brought up in a quasi-religious household I recall, as a boy, singing a hymn with the verse:

> *The rich man in his castle*
> *The poor man at his gate,*
> *He made them high and lowly*
> *And ordered their estate.*

This was then followed by the chorus:

> *All things bright and beautiful*
> *All creatures great and small*
> *All things wise and wonderful*
> *The Lord God made them all.*

(Cecil Frances Alexander, 1848)

At the time I sang it with relish, not realising that the picture painted came from an era when the churches exerted a great deal of influence both spiritual and social. The idea that everyone has their place was an underpinning belief of many early philanthropists, even people who thought that education should be extended to include working people. Two early educationalists who demonstrate this belief were Hannah More and Sarah Trimmer. Writing early in the 19th century Hannah More says:

> My plan for instructing the poor is very limited and very strict. They learn of weekdays such course works as may fit them for servants. I allow of no writing. My object has not been to teach dogma's and opinions, but to form the lower classes to habits of industry and virtue.

(Broad, 1981)

Sarah Trimmer writing at the same time suggests that:

> Poor boys sent into the world without fixed principle may, in consequence of having been taught to write and read, become very dangerous members of society.

(cited in Gregg, 1962)

If education could be dangerous so too could lifting the economic and social status of the working classes or providing them with too much charity. It has been a continual dilemma of the voluntary sector. The COS. (Charity Organisation Society) in the 19th century performed a very effective function in separating out the deserving from the undeserving poor. It also ensured that even the deserving only obtained the bare essentials and would not challenge the economic and political status quo.

The Black community is particularly prone to this and as Errol Francis sees it have become victims of a 'cultural reframing of an old terrain' (Francis, 1992). Voluntary organisations can easily find themselves intervening where people cannot cope because of structural problems such as poverty and racism, but the intervention is at a personal level and stops people becoming troublesome and dangerous. It is very important that Black communities keep their concentration on rights, politics and social action and do not get sucked into becoming merely service providers. The best examples of the Black voluntary sector at work demonstrate both the capacity to provide a sensitive and relevant service plus the vigour to campaign, educate and initiate change.

However active and effective in promoting improvements in social policy and community services, it is hard not to conclude that in a market-orientated society voluntary organisations are secondary social systems. Nicholas Deakin sees their characteristics, determined by a market orientated approach, as 'altruism, amateurism and the absence of overt political activity, with charitable status and religious affiliation as desirable extras' (Deakin, 1991).

There is an inbuilt assumption in government that the voluntary sector will acquiesce in their political and social policy planning. The whole basis of *The Individual and the Community – The Role of the Voluntary Sector*, the government's document on the role of the voluntary sector published before the general election in 1992, is of consensus and cooperation with no mention of growth through conflict. It is probably unrealistic and even unreasonable to expect governments to look for conflict and confrontation, and yet the norm for relationships between government and other political parties is clearly based on conflict not consensus.

In her review of the role of the voluntary sector Marilyn Taylor quotes Salaman in suggesting that 'the primary role for the voluntary sector is that of an instrument of government competing with the private sector in the contractual marketplace'. As a result of the Efficiency Scrutiny published by the Home Office in 1990 she considers that 'government finance in increasingly likely to be tied to specific government policy objectives rather than support for the general aims of a voluntary organisation' (Taylor, 1992).

As indicated in Chapters 2 and 5, the voluntary sector has become dependent on the financial and political climate of the moment. Numerous reports and articles from 1990 onwards record cuts in grants to the voluntary sector. One prime example of this problem relates to one of the government's verbally favoured schemes, Victim Support. In 1990 the number of Victim Support schemes supported by local councils dropped from 92 to 66 and throughout the country there were reports of local schemes 'losing posts steadily and having to cut back on services despite a 25 per cent increase in demand' (NCVO, 1990).

These dilemmas and difficulties demonstrate what can happen when the relationship between the statutory and voluntary sector becomes symbiotic. The next section looks at a different strand in the history of the voluntary sector which also needs to be acknowledged and owned.

The role of innovator, change agent and political irritant

A second strand to the historical development of voluntary organisations is an apparently contradictory role which tends to be anti-establishment rather than pro-establishment. People working in the voluntary sector probably find this role more stimulating and energising than the more passive role required in supporting the status quo. Taylor sees this as beginning in the Victorian era, especially among working-class communities when public education enabled community groups to find a voice and campaign on a wide range of social issues such as poverty, public health and prison reform (Taylor, 1992).

She sees this historical role repeated in more recent times as criticism of the growing power of professionals led to the formation of a wide range of self-help groups. Black community groups have often led the way in this respect, and demonstrate an interesting parallel with the working-class movement of the 19th century.

The voluntary sector is, of course, much better organised today than it was one hundred years ago with co-ordinating bodies for local, national and international cooperation. As one of those co-ordinating bodies in Britain the National Council for Voluntary Organisations is in a good position to take stock of the voluntary sector's effectiveness as a campaigning force. The Nathan Report of 1990 is upbeat about that role despite criticising the government for concentrating its financial support on service provision:

> The environment, penal reform, community care, human rights, overseas aid, poverty, homelessness, and mental health, are only some of the areas in which voluntary sector campaigning has challenged the conscience of the nation and strongly influenced the views and policies of Government and other decision makers.

> (Nathan Report. 1990 p.25)

The role of innovator is perceived in a variety of ways but invariably it carries a higher profile than the provision of basic or continuing services. Some commentators see this role as a privileged one that enables the voluntary sector to avoid the onerous duty of being an agency of social control or of last resort. Stuart Etherington suggests that voluntary organisations sometimes act like a protected cat in this respect:

> The voluntary sector has got used, over the last fifty years, to taking the cream; to developing innovative projects in new ways and using this innovation to persuade public authorities to develop services in a like minded way.

> (Etherington, 1989)

For some innovatory voluntary organisations talk about privilege and 'taking the cream' would seem unreal. For them being an innovator is more like doing the dirty work. An example of this is a housing advice service for young people in Leeds called 'First Stop'. When a *Guardian* reporter visited First Stop in 1991 he had to enter a blood-spattered doorstep, observe workers coping with anger and threats of violence as they tried to deal with intractable housing problems, listen to the inadequacies of statutory housing provision in the city, and hear that the project could close for lack of funding in the near future. It didn't sound much like taking the cream (Wainwright, 1991).

Innovative and irritant roles are not highly prized by government in the era of pluralist welfare services. A long era of conservative administrations with no zeal for developing welfare services let alone being challenged about it have led to a feeling of central control over both new developments and public spending. The restrictions on local authorities have been particularly pernicious in this respect. Marilyn Taylor sees the curbs on voluntary organisations as being both financial and political:

> The financial climate for agencies which speak out for the disadvantaged consumer has deteriorated considerably with the collapse of consensus politics. Legislation to curb the use of local authority funds for political publicity also constrains those voluntary organisations whom local authorities fund from making political statements.

> (Taylor, 1992)

At the heart of this dilemma is the change of language referred to particularly in Chapter 2. In a telling phrase exploring the impact of market terminology, Paul Hoggett suggests that 'we facilitate the commodification of the public sphere and the human service relationships that lie at its heart' (Hoggett, 1990).

No wonder it is so difficult to convey to statutory funding authorities the varied, complex and contradictory roles which can be played by the voluntary sector. It is safer to be a cabbage-like organisation which can be treated as a commodity.

The voluntary sector as both insider and outsider

The dilemma posed by the title of this section may seem more suitable for a treatise in social philosophy than for a section in a practical book about voluntary organisations. However, this dilemma has been part of the movement throughout its history and is one which needs addressing. The key to making use of this dilemma is to be aware of when you are at the centre and when you are at the margins. Understanding how social systems work and the mechanisms by which they direct, dictate, control and oppress is the first step. This requires some sort of access to those political and social agencies which have primary responsibility for the development of community care.

It also requires the capacity to use the experience of being on the outside and finding mechanisms for engaging with others in a similar position. Many of the individuals, groups and community associations connected with voluntary organisations see themselves as outsiders and do not take easily to linkage with semi-formal bodies. Yet here is one of the potential strengths of voluntary organisations because they themselves have to struggle to be heard. Bringing consumers of community care services into the arena of influence is an important educational and political task.

Such a task is neither easy nor straightforward. One of the creeping political features of Britain in the 1980s was the tendency towards centralised authority and power. The legacy for the 1990s in the field of community care is yet another paradox and conflict of values. The so-called 'marketisation' of community care services gives the superficial appearance of variety, consumer choice and personal freedom. In reality more powerful forces which stress order, stability and control hold centre stage. This in turn limits the capacity of the outsider or innovator to bring about change.

The role of the periphery in policy making, though not its responsibility for implementation, has accordingly been reduced.

(Deakin, 1991)

The role of the outsider seems to be largely that of provider of the most difficult kind of community service with an occasional request for a point of view about new developments. Voluntary organisations need to be arguing for a much more influential and strategic role than that, both for themselves and for other outsiders.

The low level of political support except in times of crisis

Voluntary organisations play a part not unlike that of women in a male-dominated society. They are expected to look nice, smooth over family difficulties and come up trumps at moments of crisis. They are not expected to have views of their own or make important decisions. They are not even expected to do dirty work until the nation is under threat from some outside force.

The two world wars of this century demonstrated how important both women and voluntary organisations suddenly became when it was a matter of producing enough armaments or coping with the needs of thousands of dislocated children. Unfortunately the requirements of community care and the desperate needs of many vulnerable individuals do not appear as a threat to the establishment. Few politicians actively intend community care to be a poor relation, but that is the way it works out. Community care is usually in the hands of politicians who are well intentioned but politically impotent.

For voluntary organisations working in the community care field the problem is compounded by their disparate nature. This is, of course, one of their strengths so far as choice and community allegiance is concerned, but a weakness when it comes to holding together as a political force. Deakin sees it as a particular liability in an era 'when the template of efficiency, effectiveness and economy' seems to require the voluntary sector to be a homogeneous entity (Deakin, 1991). What a paradox! A sector of community care that specialises in innovation, flexibility and adaptability is required to become more orthodox in order to have any political influence.

This failure to achieve political clout is likely to become more marked as government reduces it commitment both to the provision of services and to its financial liability. Taylor suggests that government is keen to reduce its financial commitments in the social welfare field and to encourage business, private giving and larger scale philanthropy to do more. However, charitable giving is increasingly expected to help finance education, health, sport and recreation as well as social welfare services (Taylor, 1992). This charitable giving is very unevenly spread. 'British philanthropy is most likely to go to children, animals, hospices and medical research.' Public generosity 'is not so readily tapped for drug addicts, ex-prisoners, or people with mental health problems' (Taylor, 1992).

Even in 1990 warnings were being given about growing competition for declining resources. Ken Young, the Chief Executive of the Spastics Society, was quoted in *Social Work Today* as saying that: 'The 1990s will be very competitive. Income will fall and the Government will be playing off the statutory sector against the voluntary sector' (November 1990).

The dilemma then is dealing with the gap between rhetoric and reality. In the 1992 general election in Britain all the key parties were sound on words towards voluntary organisations but lacking in political bite or financial commitment. Niall Dickson interviewed national spokespersons of the three main political parties in England regarding their policies towards the voluntary sector and decided there was little to choose between them. He also concluded that:

> It is difficult, however, to avoid the conclusion that politicians and the media, in spite of their fine words, have neither fully taken on board the phenomenal growth in the voluntary sector nor the effect this is certain to have on British political life.

(Dickson, 1991)

Community care overall and the voluntary sector's role in providing some portion of these services is dependent on social policy decisions way beyond its own boundaries. Issues about employment, income maintenance, housing and health provision are all vital elements of any community care programme.

What is particularly worrying is that there is no political party or movement striving for the development or improvement of community care, nor is it a significant issue in the population as a whole. Despite its historical limitations as a political force, the voluntary sector has to find a way of moving into the political middle ground. Part II of this chapter looks at that possibility.

PART II: DEVELOPING A POLITICAL ROLE

It is clear from the reflections in this chapter so far that developing a political role in the evolution of community care is not an easy task. However, as those on the barricades in 19th-century France realised, 'little people' should not be underestimated:

> *Be careful as you go*
> *'cos little people grow*

Perhaps that song from *Les Misérables* should become the theme tune for the voluntary sector in its quest for a more vigorous political role. However, having a theme tune is one thing, having an effective strategy is another. The second half of this chapter outlines a possible strategy by clarifying four roles and tasks which voluntary organisations need to grasp if they are to develop a more effective political role. These are:

1 Acting as community care broker;

2 Stimulating public debate;

3 Stressing the importance of collective as well as individual need;

4 Promoting a new political and moral philosophy.

Acting as community care broker

As suggested in Chapter 1, community care is in danger of becoming a political cover-up with no sector of society knowing how to confront political leaders with their responsibilities. The change from a publicly supported welfare state with collective responsibility to a pluralist, market-orientated welfare system based on individual need has let national leaders off the political hook. They can point to local government, private enterprise, the voluntary sector and a sense of family responsibility as the network now responsible for welfare services. Their role is seen merely as outlining the legislative and policy framework, leaving the operation and financing to others.

One way to confront such political neglect is to act as a bridge or broker between the *informal sector* of society consisting of individuals, families, communities and groups with special needs, and the *societal sector* consisting of state institutions, big business and central government. Being a broker is probably better than being a bridge as it implies an active role as opposed to being a passive means of transport.

The idea of being a third force is not a new one for the voluntary and independent sectors, but acting as a broker with the other two is an important development of this idea. The brokerage can go on at several levels. Within organisations it can operate as a means of empowering both the helper and the helped, between organisations it can provide a collective response when individual responses are inadequate, and when seen as an instrument of change it has the potential to place personal and community need squarely in front of decision making bodies.

A simple example may help to illustrate this potential. An individual resident of a housing scheme received continuous poll tax demands which caused personal stress and seemed likely to lead to a further breakdown in his mental health. The housing scheme worker asked for the resident's help to make it an issue within the voluntary organisation responsible for the housing scheme. This was doubly successful in that the organisation interceded with the local council to correct the poll tax demand and then promoted a local campaign in conjunction with other voluntary organisations to stop further demands being made on vulnerable people. This in turn shifted to a local lobby against the poll tax as part of a national campaign. The rest is history.

Paul Hoggett takes this idea down a slightly different path in looking for space between 'the suppressed territory in between state and market', and hoping to find 'non-market forms of co-operative production within civil society' (Hoggett, 1990, p52). He visualises the growth of voluntary, community and mutual aid organisations plus what he calls 'a range of new democratic producer organisations'. These have the potential to be:

> A virtual shadow apparatus of self-government waiting in the wings, just waiting for someone to take them seriously as something more than a set of fringe innovations – fascinating, harmless but ultimately, because of their smallness, pretty irrelevant.

As quoted in Chapter 2 he considers that the conditions now exist for a new form of collectivism, one in which a revived local government enters into a form of social contract with a wide range of community groups. Although sharing the vision which Hoggett sees, I do not think that the conditions yet exist. This is part of the political task yet to be undertaken. It is not an impossible task as it is an explicit expectation of government that the voluntary sector plays a mediating role.

> The voluntary sector occupies the ground between those areas
> which are properly the responsibility of individuals and those
> which are properly the responsibility of Government. It is an
> important and powerful third force in society which the
> Government cannot and would not wish to ignore.

> (Home Office, 1992)

A word of warning for people who see such work as the exciting cutting-edge of political involvement. Much of what is required is demanding, long-term and boring. The need to influence the Local Government Commission is a good example. The future structure and financing of local government is a crucial element in the voluntary sector's future well-being, let alone its capacity to exercise political influence. Yet, in order to get the voluntary sector's views across, regional review teams have to be presented with convincing evidence which in turn requires a lot of coordination, inter-agency liaison and report writing.

A final but important point relates to the political flexibility which will be required in both local and central government if the role of broker is going to work. The concept of welfare pluralism has dominated discussions about the provision of welfare services in general, and community care in particular. What has not so far dominated discussions in those fields is the concept of political pluralism. Marilyn Taylor puts it like this:

> Welfare pluralists also introduced the concept of political
> pluralism, where voluntary organisations are viewed as a
> medium not only for delivering services but also for giving
> different interests a voice in the political process.

> (Taylor, 1992, p150)

If this were to happen undoubtedly one of the messages which politicians would have to stomach would echo Nye Bevan's famous phrase : 'Private charity can never be a substitute for social justice.' Such hard messages are very different from the softer words more often associated with the voluntary sector. However, hard words and hard bargaining would have to become an integral part of political pluralism.

At the very least the informal, formal and societal social systems need to be interconnecting, with voluntary organisations at the forefront of communication between the individual and the state. This is only credible if all three components develop in parallel, with political awareness of its importance and political commitment through social policy outcomes. Minimalist state intervention and welfare pluralism on their own are not enough.

Stimulating public debate

In the late 1980s I heard Professor Leona Bachrach from the University of Maryland, USA, give a lecture on American perspectives of community care. To illustrate the inadequacy of relying on welfare pluralism she gave an example of an excellent project for the homeless in New York which provided 28 beds at a time when the overall figure for homeless people was 40,000. Her message was that however creative, innovative and client-centred a project may be, it needs to be developed in the context of political awareness and political responsibility.

The era of welfare pluralism is in danger of losing that sense of political responsibility. This being so the voluntary sector has to find ways of bringing debate and discussion into both the public and political arena. It has to do this as a coherent movement as opposed to a series of diverse and diffuse organisations.

The Community Care Alliance Manifesto produced before the General Election of 1992 is an example of the voluntary sector attempting to have political influence as a coherent movement. Producing a manifesto which broadly spoke for 140 different organisations was an achievement in itself. It was a demonstration that voluntary organisations could act collectively, coherently and thoroughly. What is far less clear is how much it influenced the political parties and the electorate.

This Manifesto is a good example of one kind of coherent political action. It is broadly based and as an instrument of political influence relatively soft. Are there alternative approaches that are nearer the critical, structural edge of politics which the voluntary sector could use?

Here the newer, less-established groups may have something to teach the older more formal agencies. Both Black community groups and consumer-led organisations have the advantage of having less to lose if their vigorous campaigning methods misfire. They still need good organisation and back-up, something umbrella organisations such as Councils for Voluntary Action can provide at local level, and NCVO at national level. This is where the idea of political pluralism comes into its own.

Political pluralism is not a new idea, it has been practised in China for decades in both urban and rural settings. Western democracies and Britain in particular have for too long portrayed democracy as casting your vote every four or five years in a general election and leaving the politicians to get on with it. If central government had the courage to support decision-making by local authorities, and local government had the courage to support decision making by small localities and special interest groups the voluntary sector would be well placed to assist that process.

The other sources of influence are, of course, the media. The press is always looking for a good story and voluntary organisations often have 'human interest stories' as part of everyday life. The skill is in being able to turn a human interest story into a political story. As Jane Reed of News International plc says:

> Just look at the social issues where you have first hand knowledge of how people are affected. Poverty, unemployment, homelessness, health, disability, discrimination, education, the environment.

> (Reed, 1992)

The relationship between voluntary sector workers and journalists is therefore crucial. As can be seen in so many situations journalists have not only the power to ask questions but to demand answers. Using the media more consistently needs to be a political strategy because it seems unlikely that people power on the streets will tackle broad issues of community care. The best one can hope for in that respect is where a national or local issue captures the public imagination such as the pit closures issue in 1992. Even there it required media attention over several weeks to keep the issue alive.

Stressing the importance of collective as well as individual need

The Conservative administrations of the 1980s and early 1990s have managed to convey two key messages with regard to social policy. First that collective solutions through an all-embracing Welfare State have failed, and second that individual social problems are best met by a market-led system.

Health reforms took the lead in demonstrating that this was more than an idea. The last few years of the Thatcher era showed what tenacious politicians could achieve if they put their minds to it. Both managers and clinicians have had to grit their teeth and get on with operating a market system.

Community care has been pushed in the same direction but with a much more muddled picture emerging. The emphasis from the Griffiths Report onwards has been towards individual need being assessed and services provided to meet that need from a wide range of organisations. As community care legislation has become operational, however, a needs-led system has looked increasingly unworkable.

For most people life's requirements are met by a combination of individual and collective services. A simple illustration is the Park and Ride arrangements in most cities and towns. Drive your individual means of transport to the outskirts and use the collective service to get you comfortably and without stress into the centre. It sounds easy in this example but in the community care field it is not so simple.

One of the problems is that most of the policy-makers are themselves used to seeing individual services as preferable and desirable and collective services as second class, second rate and the result of outmoded socialist thinking. A balance is needed for both practical and political reasons. Social policy practitioners such as Etherington (1990) and Heginbotham (1990) argue that there is a need for a 'communitarian' movement promoted by an enabling state which supports community action, community control and community services. This is a necessary part of any individualised community care service.

Etherington argues that developments in Europe tend towards a communitarian view, and are therefore in contrast to the British government's stance. The wholesale rejection of the Social Charter and the relevant chapter in the Maastricht Treaty reinforce this view. It can therefore be argued that the voluntary sector needs to influence government in this respect. Taylor argues that the voluntary sector has to play a part in highlighting a different perception about individual need. It involves consideration of the individual not only as a consumer but as a citizen. Such empowerment of community groups and voluntary organisations is viewed with suspicion by central government in Britain. Not only is it disapproved of, but it is impossible to combine charitable status with political action (Taylor, 1992).

In the community care arena this is an operational contradiction. Helping to set the local political agenda should be part of the role for any voluntary organisation in the community care field. By their very nature voluntary organisations have a collective focus and the particular identity any such organisation exhibits should reinforce the collective need such a group has established.

Promoting a new political and moral philosophy

To suggest that voluntary organisations should be promoting both a political and moral philosophy may bring the retort that they are getting too big for their boots. On the other hand one can argue that this has always been part of their role. I consider it part of my role in concluding this book to say what I think such a philosophy should be. It is probably for others to determine how it should be promoted.

At its centre any acceptable political and moral philosophy needs to see the individual as citizen; a citizen of the world as well as of their local community. Such citizenship would be rooted in social justice, freedom of expression, mutual respect and a sense of belonging. Czech writer and politician Vaclav Havel sees this as stemming from family commitment, community commitment, owning a sense of nationhood and finally acknowledging the need to see ourselves as citizens of the world. It is like ripples in the pond, concentric circles spreading outwards but each interconnecting and equally valid as part of being a citizen (Havel, 1991).

93

Developing a civil society

If the concept of citizenship is going to be of any value it needs to be part of the development of a civil society. This is not the same thing as a servile society. Indeed Rolf Dahrendorf would say that a civil society not only needs a plurality of organisations and institutions, (political, religious and social) but they need to be both different and opposite. He also suggests that the centralisation of political and economic power is evidence of a less civilised society (Dahrendorf, 1992).

It follows from this that the lack of authority in communal politics and in the running of local authorities is evidence of a civil society struggling against central directives. Where this occurs, and Britain in the 1990s shows all the hallmarks, organisations and communities dependent on local government for both support and finance will be both vulnerable and insecure.

The world of work is another key influence on the shape of a civil society. The world of work is dominated by large, powerful organisations with a few individuals taking major decisions. Voluntary organisations have an important role in breaking this monopoly, both in the way they employ people, and by demonstrating that work which is satisfying and meaningful does not have to be 'the job'. One of the real pressures in the quasi-market era is to resist modelling small organisations on larger bureaucracies.

Perhaps the most important feature of a civil society is how it treats 'the other' (Fuentes, 1990). 'The other' can be an immigrant worker, a deprived child, a displaced woman, a man from another race. He or she can also be a battered wife, a homeless schizophrenic, a brain-damaged adolescent or a chronic alcoholic. Whatever the label it is likely that a voluntary organisation will know the realities of being 'the other'. As a formal part of that society the voluntary sector has to make sure that 'the other' is inside a civil society and not one of the excluded.

Brenton sums up the crucial role of voluntary organisations in this respect by asking whether it is sufficient for them to be seen as 'a humane, apolitical, small-scale and cheap alternative to our over developed social services'. She answers her own question by suggesting that the voluntary sector could be involved in 'the transformation of the democratic process, where individuals and groups retrieve a sense of self-determination and begin to participate in the exercise of power' (Brenton, 1985).

Ken Livingstone argues that this was attempted in the Greater London Council in the early 1980s. Over 2000 community-based groups were funded during this time and of these 'about 80 were controversial and usually came under the categories of peace, ethnic minority, women's or lesbian and gay groups' (Livingstone, 1988). He writes convincingly that research funding for a Gay Teenage project was blocked by press and political vilification, despite evidence of distress, despair, suicide and homelessness. The lesson from the GLC seems to be that any perceived threat to the establishment, whether political, social or professional will quickly bring withdrawal of both support and money. In this instance it even led to the demise of the political body itself.

On a global scale the issues are equally worrying. The so-called victory of capitalism over socialism has left some societies without any significant element of self-criticism. Joseph Brodsky is quoted as warning that such a world would be a series of dictatorships 'in which money would be the only unifying world force and countries will be distinguishable only through their different types of exchange rates' (Fuentes, 1990). Is this the vision of a civil society that voluntary organisations want to be part of?

Finding a genuine alternative to the current system is problematic. There are some good ideas around, some of which will be explored, but where is the political power-base to come from? The phrase 'breakthrough politics' has been coined to try and go beyond tinkering or 'technical politics' (Hunter *et al*, 1992). But what would such breakthrough politics look like?

David Piachaud writing in *The Guardian* on 31st July 1991 said that significant change will only occur if central government switches it's priorities from 'an endless quest for more and more private consumption' to meeting the collective needs for better health, education and social security. For those working in socially deprived areas the market dominated era has been particularly frustrating. David Widgery, a GP in the East End of London, also writing in *The Guardian* on 3 July 1991, states that the process has been both personally and professionally harrowing: 'Partly it is what has happened to me, the grinding down of the optimism with which I came as a doctor to the

East End nearly twenty years ago, into a kind of grudging weariness punctuated with bouts of petty fury.'

Some transformation is essential. Transformation of consumer into citizen, of caring professional into social policy practitioner and of uninvolved government into government responsible for all its citizens.

From passive consumer to participant citizen

There are powerful arguments for transforming the consumer of community care services into an active citizen who will participate in decisions about those services. First, such empowerment would have a significant effect on their physical and psychological wellbeing. Second it would bring power brokers and decision-takers face to face with the effects of economic rationalism and force them to take account of social justice as a political imperative (Rees, 1991).

Where such empowerment has taken place, as in the women's movement and with certain Black community groups, the effect on the members of those groups has been striking. Voluntary organisations have great potential for liberating people from restrictive roles such as client or patient and for enabling people to develop political skills necessary to run things, take decisions and cope with responsibility. Some people only want a say in their own lives as individual consumers, while others feel they have something useful to contribute beyond their own personal needs. Self-help groups are a good vehicle for collective action of this kind but few have a real say in shaping policy.

Peter Beresford argues that such groups should now be an integral part of policy formation and considers it strange that they have not been accepted as part of the political process. He gives examples from the field of disability to show that many important social policy ideas and innovations of the 1980s came from people on the receiving end of services (Beresford, 1991).

The mental health field has also been held up as having great potential for consumer power and user influence. Liz Sayce suggests that the British mental health movement entered a new phase in the 1980s 'with the birth of patients' councils (as in Nottingham), the extension of advocacy groups (as in Milton Keynes), the advent of national co-ordinating bodies (like MINDLINK and Survivors Speak

Out) and the growth of a strong and articulate user voice' (Sayce, 1990). It is possible that one of the inhibiting factors in the transformation of the consumer has been the grassroots professional worker, both within and outside the voluntary sector.

From caring professional to social policy practitioner

As suggested in Chapter 3 the changing relationship between worker and client or worker and patient is a challenging aspect of the move towards greater user empowerment. For some of us it is difficult to let go of the assumed greater knowledge, skill and experience we carry with us and then to learn how to share expertise and power.

Letting go is the first part of that transition, finding an effective and satisfying alternative role is the second part. In practice it can be extremely difficult to empower the users of a community service without at the same time appearing to undermine the personal and professional capacity of workers in the field.

The notion of mutual empowerment is an important one as a means of thinking through the dilemma. Useful questions to ask of both parties are: 'Where does your feeling of being in charge of your life come from? What is the basis of the empowerment which you seek?'

The capacity to make choices, to influence how things are done and to take part in decision-making are all elements of empowerment. For the professional, clients are the people who give them permission to intervene in their lives. Without this permission the relationship will be negative and sometimes coercive. For clients, professionals are likely to have information, access to resources and skills in liaison with other professionals. The mutual trading of these attributes is part of mutual empowerment.

Clients and professionals can also mutually exchange the benefits of organisations. Consumer groups, self-help groups, carers groups and community groups are all examples of where the client is in charge of the resource. With their support the worker can be greatly strengthened in both obtaining services for clients and in their arguments for more resources or different policies. While still being a caring professional the worker has to become a social policy practitioner. Working together users and workers can become a formidable force.

The responsibility of the state

At the end of the 20th century there is no excuse for any civilised society not to take direct responsibility for the welfare of its citizens. This does not mean that central government has to provide directly all the services necessary, but it does mean that it has to take responsibility for enabling others to provide them. This is what that problematic word *subsidiarity* is all about. Derek Warlock, writing in *The Times* on 31 July 1991, suggests that subsidiarity was the brainchild of Pope Pius XI. He also suggests that it means providing support and co-ordination for local or regional bodies, not just letting them fend for themselves. For the British government to support the principle of subsidiarity in the European Community and then to reject the Social Charter is both illogical and irresponsible. To boast about it as a major political achievement is perverse.

Marilyn Taylor is quite clear that government has a central role both in the funding of community care, and in ensuring that all citizens can exercise a choice in obtaining services. She quotes Dahrendorf who says:

> Less government is a very pertinent political demand though it must not be misunderstood as a free pass to cut services which are needed to back up the citizenship rights of all.

(Taylor, 1992)

She argues that governments have to provide adequate funding, to take responsibility for planning and monitoring, and to ensure that local democratic mechanisms are effective. All of this has to go on in the context of a civil society committed to social justice rather than a market-dominated society which leaves the disadvantaged subject to rough justice.

Voluntary organisations have a clear and unambiguous role to promote active citizenship, to enable consumers and workers to bring about social change and to insist that whichever government is in power its community care philosophy is based on collective social justice.

REFERENCES

Beresford P (1991) 'Against Enormous Odds' in *Changing the Balance*, NCVO

Brenton M (1985) *The Voluntary Sector in British Social Service*, Longman

Broad I (1981) *A History of the Southampton Branch of the WEA*, unpublished MEd dissertation, Southampton University

Dahrendorf R (1992) *Reflections on a Civil Society*, Oxford Brookes University Sociology Society, 23 January

Deakin N (1991) 'Government and the Voluntary Sector in the 1990s', *Policy Studies*, Autumn, Vol.12(3)

Dickson N (1991) 'Different Government – New Policies?', *NCVO News*, September

Etherington S (1989) 'From the Front Line', *Insight*, 6 December

Etherington S (1990) 'From the Front Line', *Insight*, 15 August

Francis E (1992) ATSWE Annual Conference, Oxford, 23 July

Fuentes C (1990) 'The Changing World', *The Guardian*, 27 December

Gregg P (1962) *A Social and Economic History of Britain 1760–1960*, Harrup

Havel V (1991) 'On Home', *New York Review of Books*, 5 December

Heginbotham C (1990) *Return to Community*, Bedford Square Press

Hoggett P (1990) *Modernisation, Political Strategy and the Welfare State*, SAUS, University of Bristol

Home Office (1992) *The Individual and the Community – The Role of the Voluntary Sector*, HMSO

Hunter D *et al* (1992) 'Stealing up on the Vulnerable', *The Guardian*, 17 June

Livingstone K (1988) If Voting Changed Anything They'd Abolish It, Fontana

Nathan Report (1990) *Effectiveness and the Voluntary Sector*, NCVO

NCVO (1990) *NCVO News*, No.20, December

Reed J (1992) 'The Media Revolution', *NCVO News*, July

Rees S (1991) *Achieving Power*, Allen and Unwin

Sayce L (1991) *Waiting for Community Care*, MIND

Taylor M (1992) 'The Changing Role of the Nonprofit Sector in Britain: Moving Toward the Market' in B Gidron *et al* (eds) *Government and the Third Sector*, Jossey-Bass

Wainwright M (1991) 'Wolf Near the Door of Help Shop for Homeless', *The Guardian* 15 July

Select bibliography

Ahmad A (1990) *Practice with Care*, Race Equality Unit, NISW

Ahmad B (1990) *Black Perspectives in Social Work*, Venture Press

Barker I and Peck E (1987) *Power in Strange Places*, Good Practices in Mental Health

Beliappa J (1991) *Illness or Distress? Alternative Models of Mental Health*, Confederation of Indian Organisations (UK)

Beresford P and Croft S (1993) *Citizen Involvement: A Practical Guide for Change*, Macmillan

Brenton M (1985) *The Voluntary Sector in British Social Services*, Longman

Deakin N (1991) 'Government and the Voluntary Sector in the 1990s'. *Policy Studies*, Autumn Vol.12(3)

Freire P (1972) *Pedagogy of the Oppressed*, Penguin

Handy C (1988) *Understanding Voluntary Organisations*, Pelican

Handy C (1990) *The Age of Unreason*, Arrow Books

Heginbotham C (1990) *Return to Community*, Bedford Square Press

Hoggett P (1990) *Modernisation, Political Strategy and the Welfare State*, SAUS, University of Bristol

Jones K *et al* (1978) *Issues in Social Policy*, Routledge and Kegan Paul

Kramer R (1981) *Voluntary Agencies in the Welfare State*, University of California Press

—— (1990) *Voluntary Organisations in the Welfare State: on the Threshold of the '90's*, The Centre for Voluntary Organisations, Paper 8

Le Grand J (1990) *Quasi-Markets and Social Policy*, SAUS, University of Bristol

Livingstone K (1988) *If Voting Changed Anything They'd Abolish It*, Fontana

McCarthy M (1989) *The New Politics of Welfare*, Macmillan

Phaure S (1991) *Models of Voluntary Sector Community Care and Black Communities*, London Voluntary Service Council

Rees S (1991) *Achieving Power: Practice and Policy in Social Welfare*, Allen & Unwin

Sayce L (1991) *Waiting for Community Care*, MIND

Taylor M (1992) 'The Changing Role of the Nonprofit Sector in Britain: Moving Toward the Market' in B Gidron (ed.) *Government and the Third Sector*, Jossey-Bass